THE MOST COMMONLY
ASKED
QUESTIONS
ABOUT
A COURSE IN MIRACLES®

THE MOST COMMONLY
ASKED
QUESTIONS
ABOUT
A COURSE IN MIRACLES®

GLORIA AND KENNETH WAPNICK, PH.D.

Foundation for *A Course in Miracles*

Foundation for *A Course in Miracles*®
Teaching Organization of the Foundation for Inner Peace
1275 Tennanah Lake Road
Roscoe, NY 12776-5905

Library of Congress Cataloging in Publication Data

Wapnick, Gloria
    The most commonly asked questions about a Course in miracles / Kenneth and Gloria Wapnick.
    p   cm.
      ISBN 0-933291-21-3
    1.Course in miracles. 2.Spiritual life. I.Wapnick, Kenneth
      II. Title.
    BP605.C68W354 1995
    299'.93--dc20   95-2113

CONTENTS

CONTENTS

Chapter 3

APPLICATION AND PRACTICE OF
A COURSE IN MIRACLES

CONTENTS

CONTENTS

Preface

Our purpose in writing this book is to answer the most commonly asked questions that students of *A Course in Miracles* have been asking ever since its publication in 1976. Over the many years we have been teaching the Course, it has become apparent that its radical message has frequently been a source of much confusion, misunderstanding, and distortion. It is our aim in this book to help clarify, through this question-and-answer format, many of the Course's principles to facilitate greater understanding and application of its thought system.

The questions have been divided into five categories, which form the chapters of the book: The Nature of Heaven, The Nature of the Separation, Application and Practice of *A Course in Miracles*, Jesus, and the Curriculum of *A Course in Miracles*.

We would like to thank the staff and friends of the Foundation for *A Course in Miracles* for their help in formulating and compiling many of these questions, and for the students over the years who have asked them.

References to *A Course in Miracles* are given in two ways: the first cites the pages found in the first edition; the second cites the numbering system in the second edition. An example from each book follows on this and the next page:

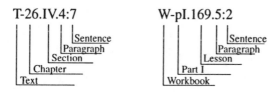

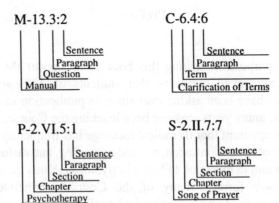

M-13.3:2
- Sentence
- Paragraph
- Question
- Manual

C-6.4:6
- Sentence
- Paragraph
- Term
- Clarification of Terms

P-2.VI.5:1
- Sentence
- Paragraph
- Section
- Chapter
- Psychotherapy

S-2.II.7:7
- Sentence
- Paragraph
- Section
- Chapter
- Song of Prayer

Chapter 1

THE NATURE OF HEAVEN

1) What is the nature of God?

To begin with, it is imperative to recognize that the true living God spoken of in *A Course in Miracles* is a non-dualistic Being, in Whom absolutely no opposites reside. The Holy One is the Creator of all life, a Being of pure Love and the Source and First Cause of non-physical reality and totality, the perfect One Who is all-encompassing, outside of Whom is literally nothing, for He is Everything. Our Source's nature cannot be described or really understood at all, as Jesus comments in the workbook:

> Oneness is simply the idea God is. And in His Being, He encompasses all things. No mind holds anything but Him. We say "God is," and then we cease to speak, for in that knowledge words are meaningless. There are no lips to speak them, and no part of mind sufficiently distinct to feel that it is now aware of something not itself. It has united with its Source. And like its Source Itself, it merely is.
> We cannot speak nor write nor even think of this at all (workbook, p. 315; W-pI.169.5:1–6:1).

Jesus states that the nature of God and His Oneness cannot be written about because it is a pure non-dualistic reality, and the spoken and written word which expresses the thinking of a split mind is dualistic. Therefore, any attempt to describe non-dualism must fail, and inevitably fall short of expressing the reality of oneness that lies beyond all expression. Again, it simply *is*. At best, therefore, all we can do is *describe* God's nature, always keeping in mind that our words are but "symbols of symbols," and "are thus twice removed from reality" (manual, p. 51; M-21.1:9-10).

1

2) What is the nature of reality?

Reality as defined by *A Course in Miracles* is not a physical realm, dimension, or experience, since reality as created by God and *as* God is formless, changeless, eternal, infinite love, and limitless and unified perfection—a non-dualistic oneness. *Reality* in the Course is synonymous with *Heaven* and obviously cannot be related in any way to the universe of form that the world calls reality. Being changeless, true reality is permanent and fixed, and therefore any thought of separation—which *is* change—is impossible and thus never was. As a non-dualistic state, reality is beyond perception, since perception presupposes a subject-object dichotomy which is inherently dualistic and so cannot be real. In *A Course in Miracles*, *reality* is also synonymous with *knowledge*, the state of being that *is* Heaven.

A representative passage from "Changeless Reality" near the end of the text provides a nice summary of the nature of reality:

> Reality is changeless. It is this that makes it real, and keeps it separate from all appearances. It must transcend all form to be itself. It cannot change.
>
> The miracle is means to demonstrate that all appearances can change because they *are* appearances, and cannot have the changelessness reality entails....
>
> Reality is changeless. Miracles but show what you have interposed between reality and your awareness is unreal, and does not interfere at all (text, pp. 597-98; T-30.VIII.1:6–2:1; 4:1-2).

3) What is the nature of life?

In *A Course in Miracles*, life as created by God has nothing to do with what we call or know of as life in the body. Life is spirit: non-material, non-dualistic, and eternal. Perhaps the clearest statement in the Course on the essence of life—what it is and what it is not—comes in this very powerful passage

from "The Laws of Chaos" in Chapter 23 of the text. It begins
with a telling and gentle mockery of our worship of the body:

> Can you paint rosy lips upon a skeleton, dress it in loveliness,
> pet it and pamper it, and make it live? And can you be content
> with an illusion that you are living?
>   There is no life outside of Heaven. Where God created life
> [Heaven], there life must be. In any state apart from Heaven
> [in the physical world] life is illusion. At best it seems like life
> [when the body is "alive"]; at worst, like death [when the
> body "dies"]. Yet both are judgments on what is not life, equal
> in their inaccuracy and lack of meaning. Life not in Heaven is
> impossible, and what is not in Heaven is not anywhere. Out-
> side of Heaven, only the conflict of illusion stands; senseless,
> impossible and beyond all reason, and yet perceived as an
> eternal barrier to Heaven. Illusions are but forms. Their con-
> tent is never true (text, p. 459; T-23.II.18:8–19:9).

Very carefully, therefore, Jesus is explaining that life is
Oneness with our Source in Heaven where the Mind of Christ
and the Mind of God are One. *Life, spirit,* and *Mind* are terms
basically synonymous with each other, sharing the characteristics of formlessness, changelessness, and eternal life. What
we in the world have identified as life in the body, such as
brain waves and heartbeats, is clearly *not* what the Course
calls life. Indeed, one workbook lesson (167) is entitled:
"There is one life, and that I share with God." Therefore, what
we experience as life, as a physical and psychological organism, is a travesty or parody of our true Self, the Christ that God
created as true life. It is important to understand how life is
seen in *A Course in Miracles*; otherwise students will end up
confusing themselves, both in understanding the Course's
non-dualistic teachings, as well as applying them to their personal lives.

4) Is the God in *A Course in Miracles* the same as the God in the Bible?

Jesus unequivocally states in the Course that God did not create this world, and thus on this basis alone He is distinctly different from the Judaeo-Christian deity. The biblical God is a dualistic creator of a material universe that he creates by the spoken word, as noted in Genesis' first account of creation: "And God said, let there be...." Thus this world and all creatures came into existence as separated entities, existing outside of him. In effect, therefore, the biblical God creates by projecting a thought or concept outside himself, where it becomes a physical "reality," as witnessed, again, in the creation story in the Book of Genesis.

But the distinctions between the two are even more profound. The biblical God is very much a person who sees sin as real, and must therefore respond to it, first by punishment, and then by the plan of the atonement wherein salvation and forgiveness are won through the suffering and sacrifice of his holy Servant (the Suffering Servant in Isaiah—Old Testament) and his only begotten Son Jesus (New Testament). The God of *A Course in Miracles*, on the other hand, is not a person and therefore has none of the anthropomorphic qualities of *homo sapiens*. This God does not even know about the separation (the Course's equivalent of the biblical notion of original sin), and thus does not and cannot respond to it.

Therefore, the God of the Course is not the God of formal religion, and certainly not the God of the Bible. In truth, our Source is beyond all concepts and anthropomorphisms, and has nothing in common with the biblical God who has all the attributes of special love (a God who has a chosen people) and special hate (a God of punishment) that are associated with the ego thought system. The previously mentioned section "The Laws of Chaos" contains a graphic portrait of this biblical God who has made sin real and thus revealed his ego origins, or better, the egos of the writers of the books of the Bible:

The arrogance on which the laws of chaos stand could not be more apparent than emerges here. Here is a principle that would define what the Creator of reality must be; what He must think and what He must believe; and how He must respond, believing it. It is not seen as even necessary that He be asked about the truth of what has been established for His belief [the reality of sin]. His Son can tell Him this, and He has but the choice whether to take his word for it or be mistaken.... [But] if God cannot be mistaken, He must accept His Son's belief in what he is [a sinner], and hate him for it.

See how the fear of God is reinforced by this... principle. Now it become impossible to turn to Him for help in misery. ✓ For now He has become the "enemy" Who caused it, to Whom appeal is useless.... And now is conflict made inevitable, beyond the help of God. For now salvation must remain impossible, because the savior has become the enemy.

There can be no release and no escape. Atonement thus ✓ becomes a myth, and vengeance, not forgiveness, is the Will of God. From where all this begins [the belief in the reality of sin], there is no sight of help that can succeed. Only destruction can be the outcome. And God Himself seems to be siding with it, to overcome His Son (text, p. 456; T-23.II.6:1-4,6; 7:1-3,5-6; 8:1-5).

This portrait, as is clear, is not only of the archetypal ego god that lies at the heart of every one's mind who believes in separation, but is also what has been so powerfully expressed in the Bible, both Old and New Testaments. This god is a figure, to make the point again, who believes in the reality of sin and in its atonement through punishment, the principal components of which—suffering and sacrifice—become the great plan of salvation or redemption. And as *A Course in Miracles* teaches, once belief in separation is accorded any reality, it is inevitable in the wrong-minded ego thought sys- ✓ tem that the ego's god be perceived as an avenger. This reflects the ego's "unholy trinity" of sin, guilt, and fear: The ego ✓ thought system posits the separation as accomplished, and calls it *sin*. Then the psychological experience of sin follows and *guilt* is born. And now the ego god demands punishment, the origin of *fear* as we have already seen in the above quotation. And behind all this insanity remains the true God of Love, Who simply "waits" for the minds of His sleeping children to awaken from their nightmare dreams and return to Him Whom they never left.

5) If God is not a person, why does Jesus portray Him that way? This is confusing.

This question goes to the heart of a very important issue for students of *A Course in Miracles*: Jesus' metaphoric use of language. It is a source of great misunderstanding for students, both in terms of understanding what Jesus is teaching in the Course, as well as in applying its principles in their everyday lives. The language of the Course is clearly dualistic, symbolic, and metaphoric—as indeed all language must be—and there are numerous places in the Course where Jesus explains that he must use the language of illusion—i.e., duality—in order for his students to understand the truths he is teaching. He says, for example, in the context of the newly born holy relationship:

> Of all the messages you have received and failed to understand, this course alone is open to your understanding and can be understood. This is *your* language. You do not understand it yet only because your whole communication is like a baby's. The sounds a baby makes and what he hears are highly unreliable, meaning different things to him at different times. Neither the sounds he hears nor sights he sees are stable yet.... Yet a holy relationship, so recently reborn itself from an unholy relationship, and yet more ancient than the old illusion it has replaced, is like a baby now in its rebirth. Still in this infant is your vision returned to you, and *he will speak the language you can understand* (text, p. 437; T-22.I.6:1-5; 7:2-3; italics ours in 7:3).

We all have experienced this same need Jesus is describing here. When speaking with children we use words and concepts that are appropriate to the child's level of understanding. Even if the *form* of what we say is not always literally true, the *content* of our love and desire to be helpful is truly genuine.

And later in the text, speaking of the Oneness of Christ that teaches us from within our separated minds, Jesus makes the same point:

> Since you believe that you are separate, Heaven presents itself to you as separate, too. Not that it is in truth, but that the link that has been given you to join the truth may reach to you through what you understand.... *Yet must It* [Oneness] *use the language that this mind can understand, in the condition in which it thinks it is* [the dualistic state of separation]. And It must use all learning to transfer illusions to the truth, taking all false ideas of what you are, and leading you beyond them to the truth that *is* beyond them (text, pp. 483-84; T-25.I. 5:1-2; 7:4-5; italics ours in 7:4).

Since, as we have already seen, there is no way Jesus can communicate to us what God our Creator and Source truly is like, he must resort to the language of myth and metaphor. These are the symbols that we—identified as bodies—*can* understand. And so throughout *A Course in Miracles*, God is referred to as a body since we cannot even think of Him without one (text, p. 364; T-18.VIII.1:7). He is called "Father," and portrayed with Arms, Hands, and a Voice, and having feelings of loneliness and incompletion. It is even implied that God has tear ducts, since He cries over His Sons who are separated from Him. Clearly, the non-dualistic God we have described cannot possess these traits or bodily parts. Moreover, the true God does not think, as *we* experience thinking. Nor can He really have a plan of Atonement as a response to the illusion of separation when, as described in the Course, He creates the Holy Spirit. The apparent contradiction here is resolved when we understand, again, that Jesus is speaking to us on the

anthropomorphic level we can understand, a wonderful example of the principle he enunciates early in the text:

√   ...a miracle, to attain its full efficacy, must be expressed in a
     language that the recipient can understand without fear (text,
     p. 20; T-2.IV.5:3).

Students of *A Course in Miracles* must be wary of falling
into the trap of taking literally what is meant figuratively.
√ A good rule of thumb is to recall that only non-duality is real.
In contrast, duality is the illusion of separation, as can be seen
in this paraphrase of a sentence from the manual in which we
substitute the word *duality* for *death*, a passage from which we
shall quote more fully in a later question:

     Teacher of God, your one assignment could be stated thus:
     Accept no compromise in which duality plays a part (manual,
     p. 64; M-27.7:1)

Any passage in *A Course in Miracles* where Jesus speaks of
God *doing* anything, of having any characteristics of *homo
sapiens*—anthropomorphisms—is inherently dualistic and
√ therefore is a metaphor to express the abstract and non-
specific Love of God that is beyond all dualism. Similarly, any
references to the Holy Spirit or Jesus *doing* anything fall into
the same category.
    To be sure, these are extremely meaningful passages for us
who still believe we are in the dualistic world of time and
space, but to take these statements as literal truth will ensure
that we never learn the lessons that will help us to awaken
from the dream that there is indeed a world of individuality
and separate bodies. All too often, students end up reinforcing
their own specialness and identification with their bodies by
never moving beyond the Course's language—borrowed from
the Bible—which largely consists of metaphoric descriptions
of God and the Holy Spirit as bodies and persons who interact
√ with them. Focusing on the Holy Spirit's true role as a
Thought in our minds, calling us to choose Him instead of the

ego as our teacher, will keep students on the right track of forgiveness.

For a fuller discussion of this very important topic, the reader may wish to consult the tape sets "Making the Holy Spirit Special: the Arrogance of the Ego" and "Duality as Metaphor in *A Course in Miracles.*"

6) What does *A Course in Miracles* mean by *creation*?

In *A Course in Miracles, creation* does not refer to anything physical, and therefore has nothing to do with material or artistic creation. Rather, *creation* involves only spirit, and can be defined as the sum of all God's Thoughts; infinite, unlimited, without beginning or end (workbook, p. 451; W-pII.11.1:1). *Christ, the one Son of God*, is the term the Course uses to denote God's creation. Christ is at one with His Creator, and there is nowhere where God ends and the Son begins (workbook, pp. 237-38; W-pI.132.12:4). Therefore, while God is the First Cause and Christ is His Effect, in a non-dualistic Heaven—the state of perfect Oneness—there can be no separation or distinction between Creator and created. Cause and Effect are thus indivisible and unseparated. Furthermore, God's creation must share in the non-dualistic, non-physical attributes of its Source. As the Creator is perfect, changeless, formless spirit, eternal life, and infinite love— whole and unified within Itself—so too must Its creation, Christ, be the same. Therefore, God and Christ are not bodies, nor are They physical and psychological entities with personalities. In "What Is Creation?" from Part II of the workbook, we find this lovely, summarizing paragraph:

> Creation is the opposite of all illusions, for creation is the truth. Creation is the holy Son of God, for in creation is His Will complete in every aspect, making every part container of the Whole. Its oneness is forever guaranteed inviolate; forever held within His holy Will, beyond all possibility of

harm, of separation, imperfection and of any spot upon its sinlessness (workbook, p. 451; W-pII.11.3).

7) What does *A Course in Miracles* mean by *creation as a process*?

Since creation is outside the temporal and spatial realms, it is not a process that can be understood by the human brain, conditioned by thoughts of time and space. *Creation*, as understood by *A Course in Miracles*, is synonymous with *non-spatial extension*, the "process" whereby God extends His Being and His Love in an ongoing outpouring of His Self. This is an outpouring, however, that never leaves His Mind and thus is never outside Him. Since God's creation—Christ—shares in the attributes of its Creator, Christ likewise creates in the same process of extension. As the Course explains:

> To extend is a fundamental aspect of God which He gave to His Son. In the creation, God extended Himself to His creations and imbued them with the same loving Will to create (text, p. 14; T-2.I.1:1-2).

> ... if God created you by extending Himself as you, you can only extend yourself as He did. Only joy increases forever, since joy and eternity are inseparable. God extends outward beyond limits and beyond time, and you who are co-creator with Him extend His Kingdom forever and beyond limit (text, p. 105; T-7.I.5:2-4).

The Son's creations (to be defined below in the next question) remain within the One Mind of Christ, as Christ remains within the One Mind of God. Oneness naturally can only remain as One, as this passage from the workbook expresses:

> God's Thoughts [Christ] are given all the power that their own Creator has. For He would add to Love by its extension. Thus His Son shares in creation, and must therefore share in power to create. What God has willed to be forever One will still be One when time is over; and will not be changed

10

throughout the course of time, remaining as it was before the thought of time began (workbook, p. 451; W-pII.11.2).

Again, what is referred to below as the "circle of creation" cannot be understood in physical terms, or in what is labeled as creativity in the world. Here in this world, creator and creation are separate; in Heaven they are one—a state that is beyond our understanding. The following passages from the text make that clear:

> The circle of creation has no end. Its starting and its ending are the same. But in itself it holds the universe of all creation, without beginning and without an end (text, p. 550; T-28.II.1:6-8).

> Your function is to add to God's treasure by creating yours. His Will *to* you is His Will *for* you. He would not withhold creation from you because His joy is in it. You cannot find joy except as God does. His joy lay in creating you, and He extends His Fatherhood to you so that you can extend yourself as He did. You do not understand this because you do not understand Him. No one who does not accept his function can understand what it is, and no one can accept his function unless he knows what *he* is (text, pp. 138-39; T-8.VI.6:1-7).

Forgiveness, which we *can* understand, is our function while believing we are here in the world, and is the process by which we learn to accept our Identity as Christ. It is this acceptance, again, which allows us finally to understand reality and what it means to be as God created us.

8) What are the *creations* spoken of in *A Course in Miracles*?

Creations are the *non-spatial*, *non-temporal*, and *non-physical* extensions of Christ, Who creates as does His Source. As we have just seen, it is the nature of the Love of Heaven to extend itself, what the Course refers to as the process of creation. Since Christ is One with His Creator and like Him in all things, He too extends His Love in creation, as we explained in the previous question. It is these extensions of Christ's Love that *A Course in Miracles* terms *creations*. To restate this important point, our creations have no parallel with anything in the physical world, just as God's creation, Christ, has no parallel with anything in the physical world, including *homo sapiens*. Similarly, our function of creating in Heaven has nothing in common with activity the world usually considers to be "creative," such as artistic creativity, creating a baby, having a creative idea, etc.

As extensions of Christ, the creations can be understood as being part of the Second Person of the Course's Trinity, our "sons" as it were, as seen in these two passages from the text:

> God wants only His Son because His Son is His only treasure. You want your creations as He wants His. Your creations are your gift to the Holy Trinity, created in gratitude for your creation. They do not leave you any more than you left your Creator, but they extend your creation as God extended Himself to you (text, p. 138; T-8.VI.5:1-4).

> Your creations belong in you, as you belong in God. You are part of God, as your sons are part of His Sons. To create is to love. Love extends outward simply because it cannot be contained. Being limitless it does not stop. It creates forever, but not in time. God's creations have always been, because He has always been. Your creations have always been, because you can create only as God creates. Eternity is yours, because He created you eternal (text, p. 104; T-7.I.3).

In keeping with his use of metaphor, Jesus sometimes speaks of the creations of Christ in language reminiscent of cheerleaders encouraging the separated Sons to return home, as in this passage:

> Heaven waits silently, and your creations are holding out their hands to help you cross and welcome them. For it is they you seek. You seek but for your own completion, and it is they who render you complete (text, p. 315; T-16.IV.8:1-3).

9) If God has one Son, why does *A Course in Miracles* use the term *Sons of God*?

Many times Jesus uses the plural to address the children of God who believe they are separate and many. This is another example of Jesus' flexible use of language so that he can meet his students at a level of separation or duality they can accept and understand. But this should not be taken to mean that there is individuality and separation in Heaven. In reality, as *A Course in Miracles* repeatedly asserts, there can be only one Son, since Unity can only create unity, and multiplicity cannot originate from Oneness. This is underscored in these important passages from the text and workbook:

> It should especially be noted that God has only *one* Son. If all His creations are His Sons, every one must be an integral part of the whole Sonship. The Sonship in its oneness transcends the sum of its parts (text, p. 29; T-2.VII.6:1-3).

> We are creation; we the Sons of God. We seem to be discrete, and unaware of our eternal unity with Him. Yet back of all our doubts, past all our fears, there still is certainty. For love remains with all its Thoughts, its sureness being theirs. God's memory is in our holy minds, which know their oneness and their unity with their Creator (workbook, p. 451; W-pII.11.4:1-5).

Therefore the term *Sons of God* is used for convenience when Jesus is addressing his students as they *believe* they are. On the other hand, *Son of God* is the term used to denote who we *truly* are as Christ, the Identity of Oneness we shall awaken to after our dream of multiplicity is undone.

10)Why does *A Course in Miracles* use masculine language in denoting the Trinity? Is Jesus a sexist?

No, Jesus is not a sexist, nor was the Course's scribe, Helen Schucman a reverse one. Indeed, *A Course in Miracles* is written linguistically within the male-dominated Judaeo-Christian

tradition, and uses the patriarchal biblical language on which
that tradition is based. Consequently, the Course conforms to
this religious culture by using Trinitarian terms that are exclu-
sively masculine. It must be understood, however, that the
Trinity is neither masculine nor feminine, and the Holy One
knows nothing of gender, since It did not create bodies. This
point is a further testimony to the difference between the
biblical creator-God and the God of *A Course in Miracles*. In
fact, Jesus himself speaks of his use of ego-oriented language:

> This course remains within the ego framework, where it is
> needed. ... It uses words, which are symbolic, and cannot ex-
> press what lies beyond symbols (manual, p. 73; C-in.3:1,3).

And so it is clear that the Course's *meaning* in using this
masculine language lies elsewhere. While the *form* of the
Course's words is the same as the twenty-five-hundred-year-
old Western tradition, its *content* is exactly the opposite. This
provides a good example of a principle enunciated twice in the
text, that the Holy Spirit does not take our special relationships
(the *form*) away from us, but instead transforms them (by
changing their purpose—the *content*) (text, pp. 333, 351;
T-17.IV.2:3-6; T-18.II.6). Therefore, the reader is given a
wonderful opportunity to practice forgiveness by having
whatever buried judgmental thoughts are unconsciously
present be raised to awareness by the Course's "sexist" language, so that they may now be looked at differently with the
Holy Spirit's help. In this way, a special hate (or love) relationship with patriarchal authorities—religious or secular—may
be transformed into a holy relationship, the relationship now
having forgiveness and peace as its purpose, instead of judgment and attack.

In like manner, we can understand the Course's usage of
the term *Son of God*. For two thousand years, it has exclu-
sively been used in Christian theology to denote *only* Jesus,
the biblical God's *only* begotten Son, and Second Person of
the Trinity. Moreover, Jesus' specialness was accentuated by

St. Paul's relegating the rest of humanity to the status of "adopted sons" of God (Galatians 4:4). To accentuate the point that he is our equal, Jesus in *A Course in Miracles* uses the same term that heretofore had excluded everyone except himself. Now, however, it denotes *all* people: God's children who yet believe they are bodies and separate from their Source and therefore different from Him. And even more specifically, the term *Son of God* denotes the students who are reading and studying *A Course in Miracles*, a usage clearly made regardless of their gender.

This term is thus deliberately used to help correct two thousand years of what *A Course in Miracles* sees as Christianity's distortion of Jesus' basic message, in this case the perfect equality and unity of the Sonship of God. And so in the Course Jesus presents himself as no different from anyone else in reality (although certainly he is different from us in time). Therefore, to state it once again, the same term—*Son of God*—that was used only for Jesus is now used for all of us. Moreover, the term is also used to denote Christ, God's preseparation creation, His one Son. Again, we see usage of the same *form* as in traditional Christianity, but with a totally different *content*. The phrase *Son of God* can also be easily understood as synonymous with *child,* a term which is also often used in the Course.

The reinterpretation of *Son of God* from exclusive to totally inclusive is crucial to the Course's thought system. And because of Jesus' reason for using this term, students—men and women alike—should be vigilant against the temptation to *change* the Course's "offensive" language. While such practice is understandable, it does serve to undermine one of Jesus' pedagogical purposes. It would be much more in keeping with the teachings of *A Course in Miracles* to leave the form as it is, and change one's mind instead. In these circumstances, one would do well to paraphrase a famous line from the text: Therefore, seek not to change the course, but choose to change your mind about the course (text, p. 415;

T-21.in.1:7). Therefore, since the Course's form will not be changed, students would be wise to use their reactions as a classroom in which they can learn to forgive, not only Jesus, Helen, or *A Course in Miracles* itself, but also all those in the past (or present) who have been perceived as treating them or others unfairly.

One final note on the subject of the Course's masculine language: It has long been a grammatical convention that pronouns referring back to a neuter noun, such as "one" or "person," take the masculine form of "he." Clearly, since a central teaching of *A Course in Miracles* is that we are not bodies—and so the members of the Trinity are not bodies either—the issue, once again, is merely one of form or style.

Chapter 2

THE NATURE OF THE SEPARATION

11) How did the ego originate, and what is to prevent the separation from happening again?

This is unquestionably the most frequently asked question of all, and it seems as if every student of *A Course in Miracles* has wondered about this at one time or another. We have been impressed over the years by the ingenuity with which Course students have framed this question in many different forms; yet the basic question itself can be restated in this way: "If God is perfect and unified, and has a perfect and unified Son, how could an imperfect thought of separation and division have possibly arisen within such a Mind?"

Jesus' answer to this question in the Course comes within a non-dualistic framework, and will hardly satisfy an intellectually inquisitive mind that demands an answer on its own terms. However, within the dualistic framework that we experience as our reality, the question is really a statement masquerading in question form, "asked" by an ego mind in order to establish its own reality and unique identity. Therefore, the questioner is really saying: "I believe I am here, and now I want you to explain to me how I got here."

Consciousness, being the first split introduced into the mind of the dreaming Son, is an ego state where a perceiver and a perceived seem to exist as separate "realities." Consciousness results in a concept of a limited false self that is separate and uncertain, seeming to experience an opposite to the true Self as God created It. And it is this false self that believes it is "here" and "asks" the question about its own seeming origin, thereby seeking to verify it. In truth, however, imperfection cannot emanate from perfection, and an imperfect thought of separation and division cannot arise from the perfect Mind of God's perfect Son, in which opposites cannot

17

exist. Only in a world of dreams can these absurdities, and the beliefs that foster such uncertainty lead to musings like this.

The question therefore can only be asked by those who believe and experience that they are indeed separate and distinct, and it can only be answered by someone who agrees with this premise that the impossible has in fact happened, and therefore requires and even demands an explanation. Thus, only a dreaming ego would ask such a question, since a Son of God, certain of his Identity in Heaven and awake in God, could not even conceive of the separation which is the basis for asking the question in the first place. And obviously, if in reality the separation never happened *once*, how could it possibly happen a *second* time? Therefore, once again, it is a trick question, much like the comedian's question, "When did you stop beating your wife?" which, if answered, can only incriminate the person responding.

Jesus directly addresses this question two times: The first is found in the text, where he gives a very practical answer to what was originally a question posed by William Thetford, Helen's colleague and friend, as she was taking down the dictation:

> It is reasonable to ask how the mind could ever have made the ego. In fact, it is the best question you could ask. There is, however, no point in giving an answer in terms of the past because the past does not matter, and history would not exist if the same errors were not being repeated in the present (text, p. 51; T-4.II.1:1-3).

In other words, why worry about how and why the separation happened in the distant past, when you are still making the same choice to be separate in the present?

The next answer comes in two parts, and is found in the clarification of terms, the appendix to the manual for teachers. Here, Jesus' answer is much more to the point as it addresses the pseudo-nature of the question itself, and his answer is reflected in our discussion above:

The ego will demand many answers that this course does not give. It does not recognize as questions the mere form of a question to which an answer is impossible. The ego may ask, "How did the impossible occur?", "To what did the impossible happen?", and may ask this in many forms. Yet there is no answer; only an experience. Seek only this, and do not let theology delay you (manual, p. 73; C-in.4).

Who asks you to define the ego and explain how it arose can be but he who thinks it real, and seeks by definition to ensure that its illusive nature is concealed behind the words that seem to make it so.

There is no definition for a lie that serves to make it true (manual, p. 77; C-2.2:5–3:1).

12) If God did not create the world or the body, who did? Moreover, who are we and how did we get here?

This is among the most commonly asked questions, and is certainly an understandable one. Almost all people believe that they are physical and psychological selves, living in a material universe that pre-existed their coming, and which will survive their leaving. The difficulty in understanding that this is *not* the case lies in the fact that we are so identified with our individual corporeal selves, that it is almost impossible to conceive of our existence on the level of the mind that is outside the world of time and space.

When the thought of separation *seemed* to occur, *A Course in Miracles* explains that the Son of God *seemed* to fall asleep and dream a dream, the contents of which are that oneness became multiplicity, and that the non-dualistic Mind of Christ became fragmented and separate from its Source, split into insane segments at war with themselves. As the Course explains, these fragments projected outside the mind a series of dreams or scripts that collectively constitute the history of the physical universe. On an individual level, the serial dramas our ego personalities identify as our own personal lives are also projections of our split and fragmented minds.

✓   Thus we are all actors and actresses on the stage of life, as
Shakespeare wrote, living out a dream that we experience as
our individual reality, separate and apart from Who we really
are as Christ. Moreover, our minds have projected many different personalities in the collective dream of the fragmented
Son, complicating the whole process. Therefore, the question
"How did we get here?" must be understood from this perspective of the collective and individual dream. In other
words, we are not truly here, but are dreaming that we are. As
A Course in Miracles states: "[We] are at home in God, dreaming of exile" (text, 169; T-10.I.2:1). And this is how the dream
seemed to happen:

> Into eternity, where all is one, there crept a tiny, mad idea, at
> which the Son of God remembered not to laugh. In his forget-
> ting [to laugh] did the thought become a serious idea, and pos-
> sible of both accomplishment and real effects (text, p. 544;
> T-27.VIII.6:2-3).

These "real effects" constitute the physical world we think is
our home. The following passage is perhaps the best description in the Course of the process whereby this effect came into
existence, once the Son took seriously the tiny, mad idea that
there could be a substitute for the Love of God. As we shall
now see, this resulted in the making of the physical universe
which is believed to be an opposite to Heaven:

> You who believe that God is fear made but one substitu-
> tion. It has taken many forms, because it was the substitution
> of illusion for truth; of fragmentation for wholeness. It has
> become so splintered and subdivided and divided again, over
> and over, that it is now almost impossible to perceive it once
> was one, and still is what it was. That one error, which
> brought truth to illusion, infinity to time, and life to death,
> was all you ever made. Your whole world rests upon it.
> Everything you see reflects it, and every special relationship
> that you have ever made is part of it.
> You may be surprised to hear how very different is reality
> from what you see. You do not realize the magnitude of that

one error. It was so vast and so completely incredible that from it a world of total unreality *had* to emerge. What else could come of it? Its fragmented aspects are fearful enough, as you begin to look at them. But nothing you have seen begins to show you the enormity of the original error, which seemed to cast you out of Heaven, to shatter knowledge into meaningless bits of disunited perceptions, and to force you to make further substitutions.

That was the first projection of error outward. The world arose to hide it, and became the screen on which it was projected and drawn between you and the truth. For truth extends inward, where the idea of loss is meaningless and only increase is conceivable. Do you really think it strange that a world in which everything is backwards and upside down arose from this projection of error? It was inevitable (text, pp. 347-48; T-18.I.4:1–6:5).

But *A Course in Miracles* further states that the world was made as an attack on God (workbook, p. 403; W-pII.3.2:1), and this was accomplished, again, by the collective split mind of the Son that believed in its hallucinatory dreaming that it had usurped First Cause. This is the beginning of the ego's unholy trinity that was mentioned above in question 4 on page 4. The guilt over his seeming sin of separation and usurpation demanded that the Son be punished. Consequently, the fearful Son sought to flee from his own insane projection of a wrathful, vengeful god who wished to destroy him. Therefore the Son projected his illusory guilt and fragmented self out of the mind, thereby miscreating a physical world of time and space in which he could hide from the non-physical god he believed he had dethroned and destroyed. Within these multiple dreams, the one Son appeared to split into billions of fragments, each of which became encased in a body of individual insane dreams, believing that this would render personal "protection" against the ego's image of a wrathful god's ultimate punishment.

It is important to note still again that we are speaking about the *collective* mind of the separated Son as the maker of the world. Every seemingly separated fragment is but a split-off part of that original one mind that sought to replace the One Mind of Christ. Thus, the individual fragment is not responsible for the world, but it *is* responsible for its belief in the reality of the world.

13) Does *A Course in Miracles* really mean that God did not create the *entire* physical universe?

We answer this question with a resounding affirmative! Since nothing of form, matter, or substance can be of God, then *nothing* of the physical universe can be real, and there is no exception to this. Workbook Lesson 43 states, in the context of perception, which is the realm of duality and separation:

> Perception is not an attribute of God. His is the realm of knowledge....In God you cannot see. Perception has no function in God, and does not exist (workbook, p. 67; W-pI.43.1:1-2; 2:1-2).

In the clarification of terms we find the following crystal clear statement about the illusory nature of the world of perception, which God did *not* create:

> The world you see is an illusion of a world. God did not create it, for what He creates must be eternal as Himself. Yet there is nothing in the world you see that will endure forever. Some things will last in time a little while longer than others [e.g., the greater cosmos, as we shall see below in a passage from the text]. But the time will come when all things visible will have an end (manual, p. 81; C-4.1).

And finally, a similar statement in the text:

> God's laws do not obtain directly to a world perception rules, for such a world could not have been created by the Mind to which perception has no meaning. Yet are His laws

reflected everywhere [through the Holy Spirit]. *Not that the world where this reflection is, is real at all.* Only because His Son believes it is, and from His Son's belief He could not let Himself be separate entirely. *He could not enter His Son's insanity with him*...(text, p. 487; T-25.III.2; italics ours).

These passages are important, because they clarify a source of misunderstanding for many students of *A Course in Miracles* who maintain that Jesus is teaching that God did in fact create the world. They assert that all the Course is teaching is that he did not create our *misperceptions* of it. Statements which contain the phrase "the world you see," as in the above passage from the manual for teachers, do not apply simply to the world we perceive through our wrong-minded lens, but rather to the fact that we *see* at all. Again, the *entire* physical universe, the world of perception and form, is illusory and outside the Mind of God.

Therefore, nothing that can be observed—nothing that has form, physicality, moves, changes, deteriorates, and ultimately dies—is of God. *A Course in Miracles* is unequivocal about this, which is why we speak of it as being a *perfect* non-dualistic thought system: It contains no exceptions. And so the seeming majesty of the cosmos and perceived glory of nature are all expressions of the ego's thought system of separation, as we see in this wonderful passage from the text:

What *seems* eternal all will have an end. The stars will disappear, and night and day will be no more. All things that come and go, the tides, the seasons and the lives of men; all things that change with time and bloom and fade will not return. Where time has set an end is not where the eternal is (text, p. 572; T-29.VI.2:7-10).

To attempt to make an exception to this fact is to attempt a compromise with truth, exactly what the ego wants in order to establish its own existence. As Jesus states in the workbook: "What is false is false, and what is true has never changed" (workbook, p. 445; W-pII.10.1:1). And again in the text:

23

How simple is salvation! All it says is what was never true is not true now, and never will be. The impossible has not occurred, and can have no effects. And that is all (text, p. 600; T-31.I.1:1-4).

In conclusion, therefore, no aspect of the illusion can be accorded truth, which means that absolutely nothing in the material universe has come from God, or is even known by Him. His reality is totally outside the world of dreams.

14) What about the beauty and goodness in the world?

Following the above answer, we can see that the so-called positive aspects of our world are equally as illusory as the negative ones. They are both aspects of a dualistic perceptual universe, which but reflect the dualistic split in the mind of the Sonship. The famous statement "Beauty is in the eye of the beholder" is also applicable here, since what one deems as beauty, another may find to be aesthetically displeasing, and vice versa. Similarly, what one society judges as good, another may judge as bad and against the common good. This can be evidenced by a careful study of history, sociology, and cultural anthropology. Therefore, using the criterion for reality of eternal changelessness that Jesus employs in the Course, we can conclude that nothing that the world deems beautiful or good is real, and so it cannot have been created by God.

Therefore, given that both beauty and goodness are relative concepts and thus are illusory, we should follow Jesus' injunction to always ask ourselves: "What is the meaning of what I behold?" (text, p. 619; T-31.VII.13:5). In other words, even though something beautiful is illusory, it remains neutral, like everything else in the world. Given to the ego, it serves its unholy purpose of reinforcing separation, specialness, and guilt. Given to the Holy Spirit, on the other hand, it serves the holy purpose of leading us to an experience of truth that lies beyond perception. For example, a sunset can reinforce the belief that I can find peace and well-being only while in its presence, or it can help remind me that the true beauty of Christ is my Identity, and that this beauty is internal, within my mind and independent of anything outside it.

15) Since we have made ourselves separate, how come we all seem to perceive the same attributes of matter, and agree on its basic characteristics and experience its laws?

When the thought of separation seemed to occur, it was a single thought in a single split mind. As the thought process of separation proceeded, culminating in the making of the physical universe, this one thought appeared to divide into billions and billions of fragments. Each of these fragments contains all aspects of the original thought of separation. Therefore, each seeming fragment would experience all the effects from that illusory thought of separation, i.e., all the so-called laws of astronomy, physics, chemistry, biology, etc., that are an inherent part of the making of the universe. Thus the *one* ego thought appears as *many*. This accounts for the paradox of people on the one hand sharing a common perception of the world, while on the other having very personal and individualized tastes, perceptions, and experiences. In the end, all seemingly separated minds are one—one thought of separation—yet each fragment *appears* to be separate, and believes itself to be unique and independent of the others.

16) What is *A Course in Miracles'* view of time?

From the perspective of *A Course in Miracles*, all of time has already occurred, even though "it seems to have a future still unknown to us" (workbook, p. 291; W-pI.158.3:7). In order to understand the Course, it is vital to get a glimpse of the view of time that Jesus is presenting. Otherwise, it will be very difficult to understand the metaphysics and its application. As he clearly states in this passage from the manual for teachers:

In order to understand the teaching-learning plan of salvation [the plan of the Atonement], it is necessary to grasp the concept of time that the course sets forth (manual, p. 4; M-2.2:1).

When we accepted the belief in our minds (before there were bodies) that we could be our own creator—i.e., self-created—we set into motion a series of cause and effect relationships. The easiest way to understand this is to consider that if we entertained the thought that we could make an opposite to Heaven, one of the effects of this thought would be the beginning of a dreamworld of time and space, and all the ways that we would manifest the effects of that thought; for example, all the many scripts of our various so-called lifetimes.

Another analogy is that an effect of that insane thought produced a dream-hologram of hatred, which has time and space as its template. Therefore, it is important to recognize that once the mind of the Sonship seemed to fall asleep, it entertained thoughts that were opposite to what truly is. For example:

Reality	Illusion
eternity	time
life	death
changelessness	change
perfection	imperfection
love	hate
limitlessness	limitation
spirit	body
formlessness	form

Hence, all the effects that the thought of separation engendered have already occurred, as well as the correction of the

Holy Spirit for every misthought. As the Course states: "This world was over long ago" (text, p. 547; T-28.I.1:6). And we are simply "reviewing mentally what has gone by," for "the script is written" (workbook, p. 291; W-pI.158.4:5,3). These two "scripts" can be likened to two holograms—the holograms of hatred and correction—which are shown in the diagram below. The part of the mind that chooses between these two is the decision maker.

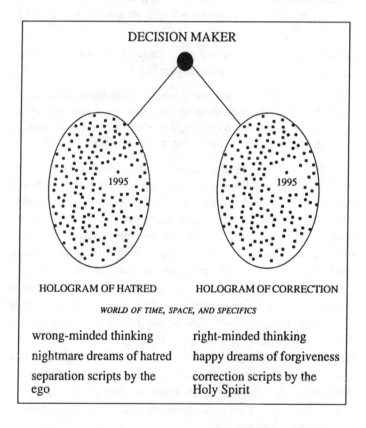

The following important passage from the text explains these two holograms:

God gave His Teacher* [the Holy Spirit] to replace the one you made, not to conflict with it. And what He would replace has been replaced. Time lasted but an instant in your mind, with no effect upon eternity. And so is all time past, and everything exactly as it was before the way to nothingness was made. *The tiny tick of time in which the first mistake was made, and all of them within that one mistake, held also the Correction for that one, and all of them that came within the first.* And in that tiny instant time was gone, for that was all it ever was. What God gave answer to is answered and is gone (text, p. 511; T-26.V.3; italics ours).

The Course's understanding of time and space is summarized in the following passage from the text:

For time and space are one illusion, which takes different forms. If it has been projected beyond your mind you think of it as time. The nearer it is brought to where it is, the more you think of it in terms of space (text, p. 519; T-26.VIII.1:3-5).

The "one illusion" is the belief in the separation from God, and it is this thought that underlies the entire physical universe that appears to span billions of years, and an almost infinite number of miles. Yet since ideas leave not their source (workbook, p. 311; W-pI.167.3:6-7), the seemingly vast universe is still the manifestation of this simple, single thought, always remaining within the split mind that conceived it in madness.

It is an integral part of the ego's strategy to keep this thought of separation protected—"the tiny, mad idea" that never truly happened—by projecting it from the mind so that the Son could never undo it by turning to the presence of the Holy Spirit Who is also in his mind. If the Son forgets he has a mind, and therefore is no longer in contact with his mind's decision to be separate, then there is no way he can ever change his mind. This is the ultimate goal in the ego's plot to sustain its own existence.

---

* See question 5 on page 6 for a discussion of the Course's use of metaphoric language, as expressed here in the phrase "God gave His Teacher."

Therefore, when the thought of separation is projected "far away" from the mind of the Son, it is expressed in the dimension of time: The past, the seeming present, and the future do appear to reflect the huge gap of billions of years the ego wishes to introduce between the mind's decision to be separate from God and the Holy Spirit, and the Son's experience of himself as a body. When the thought of separation is experienced between an individual and another person—i.e., closer to his experience of himself—then it is known as space, the physical gap we experience between ourselves and others in our special relationships. To state this another way, time (and therefore space as well) was specifically made by the ego to keep cause (the mind and its thoughts) and effect (our pain and suffering) separated. Thus, there is now a huge gap in our experience between the mind's decision to be separate, and the multiple scripts of different dreams where we experience pain and suffering as figures in these dreams. Only when cause and effect are brought together and therefore undone, can there be true healing; i.e., when the figure I call myself awakens from the dream of separation and accepts the Atonement.

In conclusion, therefore, we can understand that the world of time (and also of space) is nothing more than the projection and expression in form—*outside* the Son's mind—of the thought of separation that remains concealed *within* the Son's mind, cleverly hidden behind the defense of time and space.

17) Can the ego mind be equated with the human brain?

No. The mind is non-physical and non-tangible; i.e., it cannot be dissected in a laboratory, photographed by a camera, or analyzed by any empirical method. The brain, on the other hand, is a physical organ that is quite tangible, and can be dissected and studied readily in a laboratory. It is the "computer" that *seems* to run the body, organizing the sensory data that enter it into seemingly meaningful patterns, and directing all the bodily systems and functions to adjust to the body's place in the physical universe. In truth, however, it is the mind that is the programmer and directs the brain to function as it sees fit, just as a computer does what the operator tells it to do. The mind is the command center from which all directives emanate, as they instruct the brain to establish as an experiential reality the world of time and space that is already over, and which in truth never even existed!

In and of itself, therefore, the brain can do nothing, because it is nothing but the receptor-organ of the mind. This insane belief that the brain can function independently of the mind— which is crucial to the ego's strategy of protecting the split mind and therefore itself—is reflected in this passage from the workbook:

> You...believe the body's brain can think. If you but understood the nature of thought, you could but laugh at this insane idea. It is as if you thought you held the match that lights the sun and gives it all its warmth; or that you held the world within your hand, securely bound until you let it go. Yet this is no more foolish than to believe the body's eyes can see; the brain can think (workbook, p. 157; W-pI.92.2).

The relationship of the brain to the mind, of effect to cause, is stated here in the text:

> The brain cannot interpret what your vision sees [based upon reason, or the Holy Spirit's Presence in the mind].... The brain interprets [only] to the body, of which it is a part (text, p. 436; T-22.I.2:7,9).

Clearly then, it is the mind that does the true interpreting, not the brain. This is underscored in this passage from the manual for teachers, where the cause of perception is seen to be the mind, not the eyes nor, by implication, the brain. This passage, incidentally, is not found in the first edition of the Course:

> Yet it is surely the mind that judges what the eyes behold [not the brain]. It is the mind that interprets the eyes' messages and gives them "meaning."...Its hierarchy of values is projected outward, and it sends the body's eyes to find it.... Yet it is not

the messages they bring on which perception rests. Only the mind evaluates their messages, and so only the mind is responsible for seeing. It alone decides whether what is seen is real or illusory, desirable or undesirable, pleasurable or painful (M-8.3:3-4,7,9-11).

18) Where is the mind?

Mind, as taught in *A Course in Miracles* and as we have just seen, is non-corporeal or non-material, unlike the brain. Therefore it is invisible and intangible. Since it is also non-spatial and non-temporal, it is impossible to answer this question, which rests on the assumption that time and space *are* real. The very word *where* connotes a spatial dimension, which is unknown to the mind. Therefore, to answer this question would be to deny the very nature of the mind, and reinforce the belief that the body is real and independent of the mind which projected it and is its true cause.

19) How can one access the mind so that the mind can be changed?

In a sense, the purpose of *A Course in Miracles* is to help us do just that. The cornerstone on which the ego thought system rests is our unforgiven guilt. This roots us in our physical and psychological experience as a body and an individual personality. Thus, the ego's goal is to "protect" the guilt in our minds from being undone. As it is this guilt in our minds that is the programmer of our individual lives, so it is this guilt that must be undone through forgiveness, the Course's central teaching.

As forgiveness removes this unconscious guilt and we shift from wrong-mindedness to right-mindedness, we allow the Holy Spirit to be our programmer. Thus, His Love and peace are mediated through our minds and become our guides, instead of the ego's thought system of fear and hatred. The ego always strives to have us adopt some *new system* it has invented, such as the contemporary self-help techniques, to reprogram our "minds," so that our brains would then function to "fix up" and reprogram our lives. In this way, we become further enmeshed in the grip of the ego thought system, even though we are not aware consciously that this is what we are doing. However, we should note that it was just this belief that we are self-created and on our own, and could accomplish things by ourselves, that led to the separation in the first place. Moreover, all thought would have this as its basic pattern and goal.

The important Course principle of "a little willingness" to ask the Holy Spirit for help in order for our perceptions of ourselves and others to be corrected, imbues us with a sense of humility. This culminates in the realization that we do not know our own best interests, regardless of what the ego thought system propounds and teaches us. Thus, it is one's own responsibility to acknowledge that in order to become right-minded and remain that way, one must always access the Holy Spirit.

Even more specific is Jesus' injunction in *A Course in Miracles* that his students *look* at their egos without judgment. This *is* the way to access the mind. If students, with Jesus' love beside them, can look without judgment and guilt at their egos in action, then *who* is doing the looking? It cannot be the ego itself, but the mind—or better, the decision maker in our minds—that is *not* in the body and therefore, again, is not the ego. The following passage from the text provides a very clear description of this process and how central Jesus believes it is to the practice of his Course:

> No one can escape from illusions unless he looks at them, for not looking is the way they are protected. There is no need to shrink from illusions, for they cannot be dangerous. We are ready to look more closely at the ego's thought system because together we have the lamp that will dispel it, and since you realize you do not want it, you must be ready. Let us be very calm in doing this, for we are merely looking

honestly for truth. The "dynamics" of the ego will be our lesson for a while, for we must look first at this to see beyond it,
since you have made it real. We will undo this error quietly
together, and then look beyond it to truth.

What is healing but the removal of all that stands in the
way of knowledge? And how else can one dispel illusions
except by looking at them directly, without protecting them?
(text, p. 188; T-11.V.1:1–2:2)

And in this succinct sentence, also from the text, we find the
goal of this process clearly enunciated:

This is a crucial period in this course, for here the separation of you and the ego must be made complete (text, p. 440;
T-22.II.6:1).

The "you" is the decision maker, the part of our split minds
that chooses, which has now shifted its identification from the
ego (the wrong mind) to the Holy Spirit (the right mind).

20) What is meant by the *Sonship,* and who or what is included?

The term *Sonship,* or *Son of God* in the Course is used in
two ways: to denote the states of reality and illusion. In
Heaven, *Sonship* refers to God's one creation, the Christ Who
is God's one Son. That Son, as we have already seen, is totally
unified and at one with Himself and with His Creator. On the
level of the dream, *Sonship* refers to all parts of the one split
mind that believed it could accomplish the separation,
wherein each fragment appears to have a form and "life" of its
own. Thus, the so-called animal, vegetable, and mineral
kingdoms are all as much a part of the Sonship as is *homo
sapiens.* Distinctions of what is animate and inanimate were
arbitrarily introduced by *homo sapiens,* following the ego's
teachings, in order to be able to categorize and control an illusory world and to have "dominion over every living thing"
(Genesis 1:26,28). Such a belief is what *A Course in Miracles*
refers to as the first law of chaos, that there is a "hierarchy of

illusions" (text, p. 455; T-23.II.2:3) wherein some aspects of the illusion are considered to be higher, more evolved, or more spiritually inclined than others, as when scientists speak of the "chain of being," for example, where, by implication, there is a range of life and non-life. In fact, however, all the *forms* of "life" are the same, because they *all* are equal in their being projections of the ego thought of life-apart-from-God. This is the defense against the thought (or memory) of Life that is held by the Holy Spirit in the minds of all the seeming fragments. This is what is meant by the following passage, given in the form of a prayer from Jesus to God our Father:

> I thank You, Father, knowing You will come to close each little gap that lies between the broken pieces of Your holy Son. Your holiness, complete and perfect, lies in every one of them [through the Holy Spirit]. And they are joined because what is in one is in them all. How holy is the smallest grain of sand, when it is recognized as being part of the completed picture of God's Son! *The forms the broken pieces seem to take mean nothing. For the whole is in each one. And every aspect of the Son of God is just the same as every other part* (text, p. 557; T-28.IV.9; italics ours).

The thought of the separated Son in the mind, therefore, is not *form*, but *content*. And this is the thought that one could be separate from one's Creator, and independent of Him. The *form* this thought takes—animate or inanimate, a single-celled organism or mammal—is irrelevant, because the thought remains the same. And beyond each thought is the Thought of God, held in safekeeping by the Holy Spirit until the instant we return to it.

21) *A Course in Miracles* **teaches that there is no death. Can this be taken to mean that physical immortality is possible?**

Absolutely not! The Course teaches there is no death because spirit is immortal. The workbook lesson "I am as God created me" occurs three times and is also the central theme of a review section. This highlights the importance of the concept that only what God created (Christ) is eternal, and that this world of bodies—having been made as the opposite to Heaven—would have as its agenda to render immortality impossible. As is stated early in the text of the ego's inability to reach "eternalness":

> The ego thinks it is an advantage not to commit itself to anything that is eternal, because the eternal must come from God. Eternalness is the one function the ego has tried to develop, but has systematically failed to achieve. The ego compromises with the issue of the eternal, just as it does with all issues touching on the real question in any way (text, p 60; T-4.V.6:1-3).

In addition, bodies exist only in dreams—the hallucinations we call life—and therefore the length of this "life" has absolutely nothing to do with reality, let alone the eternal life of spirit.

One can thus see that the very term *physical immortality* is an oxymoron, a contradiction that reflects a misunderstanding of the theology of *A Course in Miracles* and obscures the crucial difference between reality and illusion. The concept is thus but one more ego ploy that many separated minds indulge in, thereby attempting to pervert the true meaning of the Course by making real the ego thought system and its world.

The devil can cite scripture for its own purpose, as Shakespeare commented in "The Merchant of Venice," and unfortunately the egos of students of *A Course in Miracles* can play the same trick. If students wish to support their own belief system that they (and their bodies) can be immortal, they can easily wrench statements from the Course out of context to support their desire. For example, under "The Attraction of Death," the third obstacle to peace in Chapter 19 of the text, there is the following statement under the subsection entitled "The Incorruptible Body":

> You have another dedication that would keep the body
> incorruptible and perfect as long as it is useful for your holy
> purpose. The body no more dies than it can feel....Death,
> were it true, would be the final and complete disruption of
> communication, which is the ego's goal (text, p. 389;
> T-19.IV-C.5:1-2; 6:5).

And another sentence that has been taken out of its context to
prove that the body can be immortal is from the manual for
teachers, the section entitled "What Is Death?" We give just
the single line here, and the total passage will be quoted below
in the next question:

> But what is born of God and still can die? (manual, p. 64;
> M-27.6:8)

And so students will falsely conclude that since they—as
physical and psychological individuals—were created by the
eternal God as Himself, they can never die. This then becomes
the rationale for affirming the validity of physical immortality.
The mistake, obviously, lies in believing that God did, in fact,
create them as individuals, and as bodies to boot. What is truly
"born of God" is Christ, our Self that is only *spirit*, and it is
that Self that is eternal and can never die. The false self that
has a physical and psychological identity remains within the
dream where there is only the illusion of birth, life, and death.

Some students, moreover, use the above lines as proof that
Jesus is advocating physical immortality by stating that the
body is incorruptible. However, they have failed to understand
the context of the above passage (and subsection title) by
eliminating the complete quotation. The reason that "the body
no more dies than it can feel" and that death is not true, is that
the body does not truly exist. Indeed, the body in truth does
not die, but that is because it does not live. Only within the
illusory dreams of the Son's sleeping mind does the body
appear to be born, live, and die—a sequence that the God of
life itself knows nothing about. Furthermore, death of the

body presupposes that there was first life; otherwise, the concept has no meaning. As Jesus *also* states in this passage:

> It [the body] does nothing. Of itself it is neither corruptible nor incorruptible. It *is* nothing. It is the result of a tiny, mad idea of corruption that can be corrected (text, p. 389; T-19.IV-C.5:3-6).

What is *nothing* therefore does not (and cannot) live, and consequently it does not (and cannot) die either.

In the text we find an even more compelling passage that describes the body's absolute lack of *being*, similar to a lifeless puppet that merely carries out the wishes of its master, the puppeteer, the body's master, of course, being the mind:

> Who punishes the body is insane. For here the little gap [separation] is seen, and yet it is not here. It has not judged itself, nor made itself to be what it is not. It does not seek to make of pain a joy and look for lasting pleasure in the dust. It does not tell you what its purpose is and cannot understand what it is for. It does not victimize, because it has no will, no preferences and no doubts. It does not wonder what it is. And so it has no need to be competitive. It can be victimized, but cannot feel itself as victim. It accepts no role, but does what it is told [by the mind], without attack.
>
> It is... a thing that cannot see... [and] cannot hear.... it has no feeling. It behaves in ways you [the decision maker in the mind] want, but never makes the choice. *It is not born and does not die.* It can but follow aimlessly the path on which it has been set (text, pp. 559-60; T-28.VI.1:1–2:5; italics ours).

Once again, within the Son's dream of separation the body does indeed seem to be born, live, and die, but this is *only* in the world of illusion. For only in the reality of spirit is there truly life or *being*, and this has nothing to do with the physical *existence* which is of the ego. That is why early in the text Jesus contrasts the specificity of illusory *existence* with the abstract reality of *being* (text, p. 64; T-4.VII.4,5).

Therefore, we conclude that *A Course in Miracles* is unequivocal in its teaching that only spirit is immortal. To believe we can exist in any other state—meaning the physical —is to follow the ego's attempts to make the dream of separation a reality, in which our individual identity is secure, by having us believe in the illusion it calls life. And this attempt, naturally, is diametrically opposed to the ultimate purpose of the Course, which is to help us all awaken from the dream of individuality to our true Identity as Christ, the immortal and one Son of God.

22) What happens when we die, and where do we go? Are the near-death experiences that many people report relevant to students of *A Course in Miracles*?

The "transition" to death can be likened to the following: 1) shifting from one sleeping dream to another; 2) completing the viewing of one video tape and beginning another; 3) changing channels from one television station to another at the completion of a program, or even before its completion if one so chooses; or finally 4) leaving one room and going into another, as was taught by the great 19th-century Indian sage Ramakrishna. Since consciousness is inherent in the split mind, and not found in the brain or body (although it is experienced there), physical death is but an illusion of an end to one's mental state, which is retained at death. Despite this thought of separation being projected onto the body, it still remains within its source: the wrong mind. Therefore, one does not *go anywhere* at death. Returning to the analogy of changing television channels, one physically remains in the living room chair, even though one's attention has shifted from the location seen on one television channel to another.

Moreover, it is important to realize that what we call death does not bring about a state of enlightenment or peace. If one does not complete the letting go of the ego's thought system *in its entirety*, thereby letting go of the wrong mind,

38

enlightenment or resurrection cannot be attainable. In fact, Jesus specifically cautions against such an escapist view of death:

> What could you choose between but life or death, waking or sleeping, peace or war, your dreams or your reality? *There is a risk of thinking death is peace*, because the world equates the body with the Self which God created. Yet a thing can never be its opposite. And death is opposite to peace, because it is the opposite of life. And life is peace. Awaken [the meaning of resurrection] and forget all thoughts of death, and you will find you have the peace of God (text, p. 541; T-27.VII.10:1-6; italics ours).

A recent variation of this belief that physical death brings freedom or release from the body is found in many people's "near-death" experiences, and questions about these experiences often are raised during our classes and workshops. The reports usually include the person's experience of leaving the body and proceeding through a dark tunnel to a circle or being of light, often identified as Jesus. This all-loving and gentle presence sometimes reviews the life with the person, and then "sends" the person back to complete lessons, accept certain responsibilities, or assume an important function (always a favorite of the ego's specialness needs).

It is not for anyone to judge these near-death experiences, and it would be foolish to deny the very positive effects such experiences have had for people. However, one *can* comment on the "theology" of such experiences and the conclusions drawn from them about the meaning of life, death, and the so-called after-life, or "life after life."

The reader must keep in mind that *A Course in Miracles* states quite clearly that the mind is not in the body, though it certainly can appear otherwise. For example, from the workbook:

> The mind can think it sleeps, but that is all. It cannot change what is its waking state. *It cannot make a body, nor*

abide within a body. What is alien to the mind does not exist, because it has no source....

What seems to be the opposite of life is merely sleeping. When the mind elects to be what it is not [the body], and to assume an alien power which it does not have, *a foreign state* [the body] *it cannot enter*, or a false condition not within its Source, it merely seems to go to sleep a while. It dreams of time; an interval in which what seems to happen never has occurred, the changes wrought are substanceless, and all events are nowhere. When the mind awakes, it but continues as it always was (workbook, pp. 311-12; W-pI.167.6:1-4; 9; italics ours).

And from "Beyond the Body" in the text:

The home of vengeance [the body] is not yours; the place you set aside to house your hate is not a prison, but an illusion of yourself. The body is a limit imposed on the universal communication that is an eternal property of mind. But the communication is internal. *Mind reaches to itself.* It is *not* made up of different parts, which reach each other. *It does not go out.* Within itself it has no limits, and there is nothing outside it. It encompasses everything. It encompasses you entirely; you within it and it within you. There is nothing else, anywhere or ever (text, p. 360; T-18.VI.8:2-11; italics ours in sentences 5,7).

Therefore, when we consider such near-death experiences from the perspective of *A Course in Miracles*, we can see that they make no sense on the level of form. How can one leave one's body, travel through a tunnel, and greet a great light, if one were never in the body in the first place? Remember that the self remains in the mind and not the body, just as a dreamer's self is not in the dream, though parts of this self are reflected there. Again, this is not to deny or invalidate a personal experience, but it is to say that however valid an experience is for the person, the interpretation is purely subjective and should not be taken for "objective" truth. For example, everyone experiences the sun as rising and setting every day, and many people report very significant aesthetic and even spiritual feelings associated with sunrises and sunsets. And yet, we know scientifically that the sun does not rise or set, but rather it is the earth that does the movement: rotating on its axis and revolving around the sun. The experience is contrary to the true explanation. Similarly, we all experience the earth as flat as we go through our daily lives, even though we understand intellectually that it is round. And so, one's experience of a near-death occurrence, or of a place to which one goes upon death (or near death) does not necessarily mean that what is understood as the experience is what truly is. And again, when one looks at such experiences through the lens of *A Course in Miracles*, one would understand them quite differently: expressions of forgiveness that were projected from the mind onto the body and its world of life, death, and near death.

As we have seen, therefore, there cannot in truth be an out-of-body experience since the mind is never in the body to begin with. And so the mind cannot leave the body, travel through a tunnel, and meet with Jesus *after* having left the body. Moreover, there is a danger in believing this way, because it strongly suggests—as do many people who have had such an experience—that such peace, joy, and happiness can *only* come to a person *after* having "died" and left the body. The whole focus of *A Course in Miracles* is on choosing and having a holy instant *right now*, on choosing Jesus or the Holy Spirit instead of the ego. One does not have to die to go to Heaven, since Heaven is an awareness of perfect Oneness, *within the mind*, and nothing else besides that. The wonderful experience of forgiveness that is frequently reported can be had in a holy instant, again, without having left the body, going through a tunnel, etc. Holding up near-death experiences to be idealized and sought for (as was depicted in the popular movie *Flatliners*) actually serves well the ego's fundamental strategy of first making the body real, and then turning it into a repulsive thing. This sets up a situation in which people would wish to be free of its prison of darkness, yearning to escape into the non-corporeal light. And all the while, the ego's thought system of separation, guilt, and specialness nestles comfortably in the mind, protected by the belief that there is indeed a body that is real, and one that truly exists in the physical world.

Thus, believing in the *reality* of such experiences is the very compromise with truth—giving light *and* darkness equal power and reality—that Jesus cautions against in *A Course in Miracles*. We see a clear statement of such a caution in the section on death in the manual for teachers, and we quote from this extremely important passage now. It begins with a reference to the standard religious belief that upon death the soul is freed to return to God, or to continue on its journey as in the Catholic doctrine of purgatory. However, the contemporary interest in near-death experiences, as we have just seen, falls into the same category of not recognizing the illusory nature of the entire physical universe and of individual existence— body, mind, and what is mistakenly referred to as "spirit":

> The curious belief that there is part of dying things [i.e., a soul, or "life force"] that may go on apart from what will die, does not proclaim a loving God nor re-establish any grounds for trust. If death is real for anything, there is no life. Death denies life. But if there is reality in life, death is denied. *No compromise in this is possible.* There is either a god of fear or One of Love. The world attempts a thousand compromises, and will attempt a thousand more. Not one can be acceptable to God's teachers, because not one could be acceptable to God. He did not make death because He did not make fear. Both are equally meaningless to Him.
>
> The "reality" of death is firmly rooted in the belief that God's Son is a body. And if God created bodies, death would indeed be real. But God would not be loving. There is no point at which the contrast between the perception of the real world and that of the world of illusions becomes more sharply evident....
>
> "And the last to be overcome will be death" [the famous

42

statement of St. Paul from his first letter to the Corinthians, 15:26]. Of course! Without the idea of death there is no world. All dreams will end with this one. This is salvation's final goal; the end of all illusions. And in death are all illusions born. What can be born of death and still have life? But what is born of God and still can die? The inconsistencies, the compromises and the rituals the world fosters in its vain attempts to cling to death and yet to think love real are mindless magic, ineffectual and meaningless. God is, and in Him all created things must be eternal. Do you not see that otherwise He has an opposite, and fear would be as real as love?

Teacher of God, your one assignment could be stated thus: Accept no compromise in which death plays a part. Do not believe in cruelty, nor let attack conceal the truth from you. What seems to die [the body that had been "alive"] has but been misperceived and carried to illusion. Now it becomes your task to let the illusion be carried to the truth. Be steadfast but in this; be not deceived by the "reality" of any changing form. Truth neither moves nor wavers nor sinks down to death and dissolution. And what is the end of death? Nothing but this; the realization that the Son of God is guiltless now and forever. Nothing but this. But do not let yourself forget it is not less than this (manual, pp.63-64; M-27.4:1–5:4; 6-7; italics ours).

In conclusion, therefore, we can understand that anything that seems to live and then die, that changes, grows, and subsequently deteriorates, or that appears to be separate from others, cannot be of God and therefore cannot be real. And so all categories that relate to bodies in any way—including death and near death—have no true meaning because they do not truly exist. Their only meaning within the illusion comes in their serving as classrooms in which we learn the lesson of discerning between the meaningless and the meaningful.

23) Does *enlightenment* or *resurrection* mean freedom from the body?

No, because the mind is not imprisoned in the body, but only in its own decision to identify with the ego thought system; hence, enlightenment can be understood as awakening from the dream, a process occurring only on the level of the mind. As the Course says: "Enlightenment is but a recognition, not a change at all" (workbook, p. 347; W-pI.188.1:4). Therefore, it can be understood as the acceptance of ourselves as God created us, and the recognition that no change is necessary because in truth the separation from God never occurred. This recognition is what *A Course in Miracles* means by accepting the Atonement for oneself. Moreover, the Course's definition of *resurrection* is the awakening from the ego's dream of death, as is seen in the manual's answer to the question, "What is the resurrection?" where the process of "overcoming" death is clearly placed in the mind, since death has nothing to do with the body:

> Very simply, the resurrection is the overcoming or surmounting of death. It is a reawakening or a rebirth; *a change of mind* about the meaning of the world. It is the acceptance of the Holy Spirit's interpretation of the world's purpose; the acceptance of the Atonement for oneself. It is the end of dreams of misery, and the glad awareness of the Holy Spirit's final dream....
>
> The resurrection is the denial of death, being the assertion of life. Thus is all the thinking of the world reversed entirely (manual, p. 65; M-28.1:1-4; 2:1-2; italics ours).

And from "The Message of the Crucifixion" in Chapter 6 of the text, where Jesus speaks of himself and his importance to us as a model, we read:

> Your resurrection is your reawakening. I am the model for rebirth, but rebirth itself is merely the dawning on your *mind* of what is already in it. God placed it there Himself, and so it is true forever (text, p. 86; T-6.I.7:1-3; italics ours).

The emphasis that both these passages place on the mind clearly points to *it*, and *not* the body as the site of resurrection (or the process of forgiveness). It is the split mind that is the source of all dreams, and therefore it is only there that correction is needed and can be truly efficacious.

Therefore, one can be enlightened and still have the *appearance* of remaining in the body, as did Jesus for example, being fully aware that his reality was *outside* the dream of bodies. *Resurrection*, thus, only means freedom from the *belief* that we actually exist within a body and are a body. It is the culmination of the process, once again, that occurs only on the level of the mind, because the ego's dream of separation exists only there and nowhere else. Ideas always remain within their source, as Jesus frequently teaches in the Course, and so the *idea* of a separated world and body has never left its *source* in the split mind.

Chapter 3

APPLICATION AND PRACTICE OF
A COURSE IN MIRACLES

24) If all this is a dream or an illusion, or a script which is already written, what difference does it make what I do with my life?

While on one level *A Course in Miracles* does teach that this world is an illusion and that in truth our experiences here are hallucinations, on another level Jesus assures us that "it is almost impossible to deny its [the body's] existence in this world. Those who do so are engaging in a particularly unworthy from of denial" (text, p. 20; T-2.IV.3:10-11). Since it was our wrong minds that wrote the script of our many "lifetimes" in this delusional hologram of hatred, it would follow that the ego's purpose would be to reinforce belief in the seeming reality of our experience here, which reflects our belief in the reality of our separation from God. And nothing serves this purpose better than the defense of denial, which makes the thoughts of guilt and fear so unacceptably real that they need to be repressed and never looked at again. This ensures that the thought of separation remains real within the split mind, "safe and protected" from the Holy Spirit.

A Course in Miracles presents us with a choice between two ways of living in this dream world, which is the only *true* choice remaining to us within the dream. As we implied earlier, the Course teaches that we have a split mind which is really tri-partite in structure: 1) a wrong mind that holds the ego thought system in place, and even though it *appears* that we have choices within the wrong mind, Jesus unequivocally states that to believe that there is a choice in the thought system of the ego is delusional and self-deceptive; 2) a right mind which is the home of the Holy Spirit, and holds a correction for each misthought or miscreation of the ego thought system;

and 3) the part of the mind that chooses between the ego and the Holy Spirit, which we refer to as the decision maker. Therefore, our only true choice and freedom within the illusory dream of separation is to choose our right minds, allowing our wrong minds to be undone. We shall return to this important point in a later question.

Consequently, *A Course in Miracles* instructs us that the only purpose the world holds is for us to choose the forgiveness script. The Holy Spirit offers us a correction for the ego's nightmare dreams of guilt and attack, wherein the world becomes a classroom in which we can learn the lessons of forgiveness. In this way, the guilt we made that ultimately brought about the making of the body and the world is undone. Simply indulging the ego's fantasies under the justification that "It doesn't matter anyway" would make these desires real (otherwise why indulge them?), and root one still further in the ego's dream of guilt. Such self-indulgence could include acting out repressed desires such as murder, theft, deception, anger, sexual exploitation, etc., or on the other hand, giving way to thoughts of meaninglessness, depression, and even suicide. And thus the above question—"What difference does it make what I do with my life?"—can be understood from a totally different perspective. This is a perspective that gives great meaning to our lives, for it states: "I have a choice to make: which dream do I choose to follow; to which dream will I be loyal?"

In summary then, we see that on the metaphysical level, everything we do—not to mention our personal identity—is an illusion. However, on the level of the dream, where we most certainly believe we are, our lives make a tremendous difference; not so much in terms of *what* we do, but with *whom* we do it. Only by choosing Jesus or the Holy Spirit as our teacher, guide, and friend can we undo the cause of our remaining asleep and dreaming dreams which are rooted in the belief in the reality of the separation from our Source, and from each other. We cannot change the script, which is already written and has indeed been undone. But we can change from the ego's script to the Holy Spirit's. Helping us to accomplish this is the purpose of *A Course in Miracles.*

25) If all this is a dream or an illusion, does that mean that the abuse I suffered as a child is unreal and should be denied or ignored?

Following from the answer to the preceding question, one can understand that childhood abuse, or any victimization, is part of a larger script that came into existence with the original thought of separation, which then shattered into billions of fragments. The "me" that I experience as myself, as well as all the experiences of the life I call my own, are but one aspect of the larger script of the decision maker. Indeed, all ego scripts are but projected dreams of a world of opposites that results from the belief that we (the victimizers) could banish God and His unity (the victim) from our minds. Thus, any part of our individual lives is a congealing in form of the ego script of victim-victimizer. Moreover, I must accept responsibility that my decision maker has written a script where I would experience the pain of abuse so that I could prove that God was wrong and I was right. In other words, there is no unity of the Sonship because the thoughts of separation and victimization actually occurred. Until I can accept this fact of my dream, I will not be able to accept the correction and healing of the Holy Spirit. Most importantly, people should never deny what seems to be happening to them in their dreams, for these events become the means of helping them to awaken from the dream. Rather, they should pay careful attention to such experiences and *then* ask the Holy Spirit for help in becoming a happy learner, and accepting His happy dreams of correction to replace the nightmare dreams that their egos had made.

For example, if one suffered such painful abuse as a child that all memories had been repressed and therefore rendered inaccessible to correction, some form of therapeutic intervention that allows the person to recall the early abuse can often be extremely helpful. If this is not done, the thought of fear that "protects" the thought of victimization is accorded power, and indeed continues to exercise this power in the service of maintaining the ego's thought system of separation and pain. Therefore, as *A Course in Miracles* repeatedly emphasizes, a happy dream of forgiveness must precede the ultimate awakening, in which—still within the context of the dream of separation—a person is able to look with Jesus at the bitter symbols of the dream's past, open them to re-examination and therefore correction. This is the meaning of the following all-important passage from the text that conveys the gentleness of Jesus' corrective and healing love:

> Nothing more fearful than an idle dream has terrified God's Son, and made him think that he has lost his innocence, denied his Father, and made war upon himself. So fearful is the dream, so seeming real, he could not waken to reality without the sweat of terror and a scream of mortal fear, unless a gentler dream preceded his awaking, and allowed his calmer mind to welcome, not to fear, the Voice that calls with love to waken him; a gentler dream, in which his suffering was healed and where his brother was his friend. God willed he waken gently and with joy, and gave him means to waken without fear (text, p. 542; T-27.VII.13:3-5).

And so, any intervention that allows individuals to gain access to their fear thoughts so that they can be looked at through the eyes of Jesus' forgiveness—a vision of non-judgment—is of help. That is why Jesus dictated to Helen the pamphlet "Psychotherapy: Purpose, Process and Practice." Though it clearly occurs within the ego's dream of separation, psychotherapy can nonetheless be redirected by the Holy Spirit to serve His holy purpose of undoing the dream—through reversing the dynamics of denial and projection—by reflecting in therapist and patient the joining of God and Christ that is the only truth.

As we have stated previously, it is indeed true that meta-✓ physically speaking one's early childhood abuse (or *anything* within a dream) is an illusion, but as long as one believes it *did* indeed happen—otherwise there would be no fear, denial, anger, or pain—then help must be reflected in the form the person needs. To dismiss a problem as mere illusion when one still believes one is a body and personality is simply silly, and not a legitimate spiritual practice. Such practice in denial clearly serves no one well, and Jesus did not give us a Course in denial, but one in its *undoing*.

26) What about congenital defects or infant deaths? Are these chosen also?

A congenital defect, as well as an infant's death, is not chosen by the *brain* of the baby, but by the *mind* that projected a figure in a dream that was born deformed or died at a very early age. Please refer to the diagram on page 27, and recall that the split mind projects out many thoughts that take form throughout the hologram of time and space. Therefore, if a thought of imperfection or death is entertained by the separated mind, it can be experienced as a congenital defect or an infant death in what is perceived to be the life of an individual. If one returns to our earlier analogy of the body (and brain) as a puppet, carrying out the wishes of the *non-human* mind, answers to questions like the above will make perfect sense.

27) Are babies born innocent?

The only true state of innocence is in Heaven, the real home of God's Son. With very, very few exceptions—the Teachers of teachers referred to in the manual for teachers (manual, p. 61; M-26.2)—only those who retain guilt in their minds "come here" and are born. Workbook Lesson 182 provides a poignant portrait of all inhabitants of this world:

> We speak today for everyone who walks this world, for he
> is not at home. He goes uncertainly about in endless search,
> seeking in darkness what he cannot find; not recognizing
> what it is he seeks. A thousand homes he makes, yet none
> contents his restless mind. He does not understand he builds
> in vain. The home he seeks can not be made by him. There is
> no substitute for Heaven. All he ever made was hell (work-
> book, p. 331; W-pI.182.3).

And yet it is this very belief that there *is* a substitute for
Heaven that constitutes sin, and the resultant and inevitable
guilt continually propels the separated Son to review mentally
the thought of separation and its effects that have already gone
by. Thus all who come here share this guilt over their lost
innocence. Moreover, their egos' purpose for their manifestation in the world is the reinforcement of this guilt. On the other
hand, the Holy Spirit's purpose once people believe they are
here, is the unlearning of this guilt through the practice of forgiveness that undoes the belief in victimization. This eventually restores to all the separated ones their awareness of the
innocence that is rightly and eternally theirs as God's one Son,
the Christ He created as One with Him.

In this context, one can understand that the popular view
that babies are born innocent and are corrupted by society—
Rousseau's "noble savage" thesis—falls very nicely within
the ego's strategic plan to convince us that the world is real
and has victimizing effects on us. The ego thought system
upholds the idea that we are *not* the dreamer of the dream that
is the world, but that rather the dream is dreaming us. Therefore, it is the world that is responsible for the loss of my innocence. It was not that I gave it away by my thoughts, but rather
that it was taken from me, the innocent victim of a world I did
not make or choose. This fundamental ego principle is the subject of the following passage from "The Hero of the Dream":

> The body's serial adventures, from the time of birth to
> dying are the theme of every dream the world has ever had.
> The "hero" of this dream will never change, nor will its

purpose. Though the dream itself takes many forms, and seems to show a great variety of places and events wherein its "hero" finds itself, the dream has but one purpose, taught in many ways. This single lesson does it try to teach again, and ✓ still again, and yet once more; *that it is cause and not effect. And you are its effect, and cannot be its cause.*

Thus are you not the dreamer, but the dream. And so you wander idly in and out of places and events that it contrives. That this is all the body does is true, for it is but *a figure in a dream* (text, pp. 543-44; T-27.VIII.3:1–4:3; italics ours).

Since ultimately our lives are our dreams—the outpicturing of the thoughts in our minds—only we can be responsible for the loss of innocence that is the central theme of everyone's dream. No one is *born* innocent; only Christ is innocent, and He was never born. But through the process of forgiveness and accepting the correction for our mistaken thoughts, we can remember that we never truly sinned. In truth, therefore, we are innocent of any belief that we separated ourselves from Innocence Itself.

28) Does *A Course in Miracles* have a morality, or a code of ethics?

The answer to this question depends on how *morality* is defined. The dictionary defines the term as a set of rules or principles of conduct; a system of morals or ethics that defines what is right and what is wrong. Looking at the first part of the definition, *A Course in Miracles* does not present a set of rules on how one should act in the world, but it most definitely presents a schemata of the post-separation split mind divided into a wrong and right mind, the respective domains of the ego and the Holy Spirit.

From a historical point of view, *homo sapiens'* sojourn on this planet has been anything but moral, even though civilization after civilization has enacted moral codes that govern the affairs of the everyday life of its citizens. If the inhabitants of any society, nation-state, or civilization are operating from the belief in scarcity, the principle of lack which governs the entire thought system of the ego, the moral codes and laws will inevitably reflect this choice. And the blood-drenched events of history are witnesses to the ego's thought system of "kill or be killed" that is the *unconscious* underpinning of all the moralities of the world.

Therefore, even though a system of morality might espouse noble ideals, if its origin were the wrong mind, it could never bring about a correction for what is deemed immoral or amoral. Furthermore, how is a society to determine what is right or wrong, and who should be the ones to make such decisions? If one studies the cultures of the past and present, amazement will result when one objectively looks at what is considered right or wrong by any group of people throughout the span of time. For example, during the Inquisition it was considered the highest morality to seek, find, and punish those who did not agree with the Roman Catholic Church, whose teachings were believed to have come from God and Jesus. So, in Their Names, heretics were tortured and killed. Basically then, the group that holds religious, economic, or political power in any society, depending on whether it is a theocratic or secular state, determines what is right and wrong.

A Course in Miracles presents us with a new mode of being in this dream world that is far beyond any morality or rules of conduct to which the world pays homage. This new mode of being asks us to become aware of the thoughts of our wrong minds, and then to ask for help in switching to a correction that already exists in our right minds. In order to accomplish this, we must get our ego selves out of the way and let go of any moral values, desires, or investments in any outcomes, whether they involve conduct, rules, or expectations. The following exhortation from the workbook clearly summarizes this approach of undoing all that we had believed before, so that the Wisdom of God can speak to us and guide our thoughts, words, and behavior:

Simply do this: Be still, and lay aside all thoughts of what you are and what God is; all concepts you have learned about the world; all images you hold about yourself. Empty your mind of everything it thinks is either true or false, or good or bad, of every thought it judges worthy, and all the ideas of which it is ashamed. Hold onto nothing. Do not bring with you one thought the past has taught, nor one belief you ever learned before from anything. Forget this world, forget this course, and come with wholly empty hands unto your God.

Is it not He Who knows the way to you? You need not ✓ know the way to Him. Your part is simply to allow all obstacles that you have interposed between the Son and God the Father to be quietly removed forever. God will do His part in joyful and immediate response (workbook, p. 350; W-pI.189.7:1–8:4).

Therefore, from the perspective of *A Course in Miracles*, what is "right" is accessing the right mind and following the guidance of the Holy Spirit or Jesus; while what is "wrong" is choosing the wrong mind and listening to the insane voice of the ego's thought system of specialness. We could thus coin a new term—*non-normative ethics*—to denote the Course's unique code for living in this world. What fosters this morality is the daily practice of forgiveness, which undoes the blocks to the presence of the Holy Spirit's Love and wisdom that can flow through our minds to guide our behavior. As Jesus so movingly writes in the workbook:

For this alone I need; that you will hear the words I speak, and ✓ give them to the world. You are my voice, my eyes, my feet, my hands through which I save the world (workbook, p. 322; W-pI.rV.in.9:2-3).

29) Since all sickness is a projection of the mind's guilt, does this mean that it is wrong to take medicine for physical pain?

Absolutely not. As we have just explained, the Course's "morality"—whether any particular behavior is "right" or

"wrong"—depends only on which voice we choose to listen
to. And there certainly could be instances when the guidance
of Jesus would be to take medication or pain-killers. Above
all, as is seen throughout *A Course in Miracles*, his teaching
and guidance is gentle and loving, which is exemplified in an
extremely important passage near the beginning of the text. It
specifically addresses this issue of taking medicine, a form of
what the Course refers to as magic. The passage is particularly
important because of the tendency for students of *A Course in
Miracles* to judgmentally use its teachings against themselves
or others. It is also an excellent example of the integration of
what we have frequently referred to as the two levels of the
Course: Level I—the metaphysical foundation of the Course's
teachings that contrasts the reality of God and Christ with the
ego's illusory world; and Level II—the part of the Course's
teachings that focuses *only* on the world of illusion, the dream.
On this level, the truth is the Holy Spirit's interpretation of the
world as a classroom in which we learn forgiveness, contrasted with the illusion that is the ego's vicious use of the
world to advance its own specialness. The passage begins with
a metaphysical statement about the illusory nature of the body,
and then Jesus gently shifts the focus to the experience of his
students when they are gripped with fear:

> All material means that you accept as remedies for bodily
> ills are restatements of magic principles. This is the first step
> in believing that the body makes its own illness. It is a second
> misstep to attempt to heal it through non-creative agents. *It
> does not follow, however, that the use of such agents for
> corrective purposes is evil.* Sometimes the illness has a suffi-
> ciently strong hold over the mind to render a person tempo-
> rarily inaccessible to the Atonement. In this case it may be
> wise to utilize a compromise approach to mind and body, in
> which something from the outside is temporarily given heal-
> ing belief. This is because the last thing that can help the non-
> right-minded, or the sick, is an increase in fear. They are
> already in a fear-weakened state. If they are prematurely

exposed to a miracle, they may be precipitated into panic. This is likely to occur when upside-down perception has induced the belief that miracles are frightening (text, p. 20; T-2.IV.4; italics ours).

From a reading of other passages in the Course, it is apparent that since the origin and content of all dreams is fear, everyone in this world is in a fear state. Moreover, there is an inherent fear of the power of the miracle to release us from all defenses that "protect" us from the "threat" of God's Love. Sickness and pain constitute essential aspects of the ego's plan of protection, since they rivet our attention on our bodies and away from our Identity as spirit, the memory of which is held for us by the Holy Spirit in our right minds (see workbook Lesson 136, "Sickness is a defense against the truth"). Therefore we usually need the "compromise approach" Jesus mentions above. And so very often, a decision to ask the Holy Spirit for help instead of the ego—because of our fear—needs to be expressed in material form, as Jesus explains in this passage from the manual:

> The acceptance of sickness as a decision of the mind, for a purpose for which it would use the body, is the basis of healing. And this is so for healing in all forms. A patient decides that this is so, and he recovers. If he decides against recovery, he will not be healed. Who is the physician? Only the mind of the patient himself. The outcome is what he decides that it is. *Special agents seem to be ministering to him, yet they but give form to his own choice. He chooses them in order to bring tangible form to his desires. And it is this they do, and nothing else. They are not actually needed at all.* The patient could merely rise up without their aid and say, "I have no use for this." There is no form of sickness that would not be cured at once (manual, p. 17; M-5.II.2; italics ours).

Therefore, taking medicine can actually be an expression of students' asking Jesus for help, and accepting that help in the form that does not reinforce their fear of the power of their minds to heal. The fear is exacerbated because the ego's thought of attacking God and usurping His role as First Cause is also found in the mind. And so returning to the mind its power to decide *for* God, also calls forth the memory of its misuse of that power to choose *against* Him. The guilt acts almost as an electric grid that emits a shock whenever it is approached, recoiling us from our goal. And so often our asking Jesus for help in our minds needs to be "compromised" by mediating that help through the body. This dynamic is reflected in the following paragraph, part of which we quoted earlier:

> The value of the Atonement does not lie in the manner in which it is expressed. In fact, if it is used truly, it will inevitably be expressed in whatever way is most helpful to the receiver. This means that a miracle, to attain its full efficacy, must be expressed in a language that the recipient can understand without fear. This does not necessarily mean that this is the highest level of communication of which he is capable. It does mean, however, that it is the highest level of communication of which he is capable *now*. The whole aim of the miracle is to raise the level of communication, not to lower it by increasing fear (text, pp. 20-21; T-2.IV.5).

Even though taking medicine is, on one level, expressing the "misstep to attempt to heal...through non-creative agents," on another level—as we have already discussed—it reflects turning to Jesus for help and accepting it on the only level that does not reinforce fear. To exclude such behavior in the name of the teachings of *A Course in Miracles* is subtly to make the body real by stating that certain behaviors are "evil" or "wrong." In the words of Hamlet: "There is nothing right or wrong, but thinking makes it so." And our thinking can express either the "wrong" thought system of the ego, or the "right" one of the Holy Spirit. Our actions simply mirror the decision our minds have made. However, as we shall discuss in the next question, it is a mistake to attempt to understand which teacher has been chosen based upon observable actions.

30) Does being defenseless mean I should let someone kill or rape me, or stand by while violence is committed against loved ones or others?

We begin by stating that defenselessness is a thought of the right mind, an *attitude* based upon the Holy Spirit's thought system that the Son of God is innocent and sinless, and therefore invulnerable. If there is no sin there can be no guilt. And without guilt there can be no projection, which means there can be no fear of being attacked. Guilt, as the Course teaches, demands punishment: if no guilt exists, fear of punishment is also non-existent. Finally, without fear of punishment from *without*, there is no need for defenses *within*, and so the true state of defenselessness is the *thought* of innocence and invulnerability.

This does not then mean that a right-minded person's behavior is necessarily what the world thinks of as defenseless. The meaning of *spiritual defenselessness* is often distorted, so that people think they must be totally passive, like doormats, to be defenseless. To let others do violence to oneself, a loved one, or anyone else, very often is allowing those persons to act in a manner that would not only be harmful to their "victims," but to themselves as well by reinforcing their own guilt over their separation from God and from the rest of the Sonship. Acting *behaviorally* to "protect" oneself can actually then be following the Holy Spirit's guidance in the *mind* to be loving. It is not the *form* of the behavior that reflects defenselessness, but the *content* of the mind's thought.

Both our professional experiences offered examples of this principle. My (Kenneth's) first employment as a psychologist was working with disturbed children in a special school. These were children ranging from ages five to thirteen, many of whom had severe behavioral problems which often manifested in their acting violently towards themselves and others. I devised a way that I could control their behavior by getting them to the floor, wrapping my legs and arms around them in such manner that they were not hurt, but were unable to kick, punch, bite, scratch, or harm anyone. Thus by preventing their attempts at behavioral violence, I was able eventually to calm them down. My behavior could have looked to an observer as defensive, although obviously its purpose was only to help.

During my tenure as teacher and dean in a New York City high school, I (Gloria) many times had to have teens suspended from school or arrested for various kinds of violent behavior and use of weapons. My intervention, too, could have been interpreted by an observer as defensive. Yet, checking out my responses as best I could with Jesus as to how I should proceed, resulted in—paraphrasing from the text— setting a limit on the teenagers' ability to miscreate (text, p. 18; T-2.III.3:3). Thus they were prevented from acting out more murderous thoughts which would have resulted in a greater reinforcement of their guilt. I always felt it was my responsibility as dean, which was a dream role I scripted, to get myself out of the way to the best of my ability so that I could access the correction script of the Holy Spirit in these difficult circumstances. I had the little willingness *A Course in Miracles* speaks about, but I sometimes wondered in my early days with the Course, why I scripted such seemingly difficult situations!

For us to have acted otherwise—i.e., to have been behaviorally passive or "defenseless" in the face of such aggressive actions—would have been as unloving as it would be to let a rapist brutally assault your wife or daughter while you are standing by mouthing Course "platitudes" about not being a body, how love does not defend itself, etc. As with everything related to the teachings of *A Course in Miracles*, it is the content or purpose that supplies the meaning to our actions, and the only true meaning comes from Jesus or the Holy Spirit in our minds. Their love is abstract and non-specific, and always the same. Yet this love is expressed through the specific expressions of our individuality, and therefore differs from one person to the next. Thus, only one with the wisdom of

Jesus would be in a position to justly and fairly evaluate another's actions. For anyone else it would be foolhardy and arrogant to make such judgments. As he instructs us in the manual for teachers:

> In order to judge anything rightly, one would have to be fully aware of an inconceivably wide range of things; past, present and to come.... And one would have to be certain there is no distortion in his perception, so that his judgment would be wholly fair to everyone on whom it rests now and in the future. Who is in a position to do this? Who except in grandiose fantasies would claim this for himself?... Make then but one more judgment. It is this: There is Some-one with you Whose judgment is perfect (manual, pp. 26-27; M-10.3:3,5-7; 4:6-7).

And so the bottom line is always to ask Jesus or the Holy Spirit for help before we respond to a difficult situation, as well as to ask Their help before attempting to judge another's response in a difficult situation.

31) Can one be a student of *A Course in Miracles* and serve on a jury (be a doctor, lawyer, etc.) or remain with a partner who is not a student of the Course? Or should one be with a partner at all? Isn't that simply a form of specialness?

These questions reflect the level confusion we have already considered, for they suggest that there are certain activities, occupations, or relationships that are more or less spiritual than others. For example, the underlying assumptions are that it is holier to become a teacher of *A Course in Miracles* than it is to serve in government or the armed forces. In other words, this assumption makes the error real, something Jesus distinctly cautions his students against doing. Indeed, the first law of chaos described in Chapter 23, and already referred to, explicitly states the ego's principle that there "is a hierarchy of illusions" (text, p. 455; T-23.II.2:3).

As we have frequently stated in this book, the focus of the Course student should never be on specific behavior, but only on which voice is chosen as a guide for this behavior. Everything else is meaningless. Very often, difficult occupations provide the best classrooms in which to learn and practice the principle of forgiveness, which is based on the premise that nothing outside us can affect us in any way. It is only our minds' choices for the ego that can bring us pain. Many years ago we were giving a workshop in Albuquerque, New Mexico. A man stood up and spoke of his work at Los Alamos, site of some of this country's most significant nuclear weapons research and production. Several of the participants began to attack him for being a student of *A Course in Miracles* at the same time that he was involved in what they felt was bellicose and obviously ego-based activity. They clearly missed the whole point. What better classroom could there be for someone than to operate in the midst of such a blatant example of the ego thought system, and learn how to see it differently through the eyes of forgiveness, and especially how to see oneself differently. And is working on a nuclear bomb really any different from participation in any institution in the world, all of which deal with separation, specialness, and the perpetuation of the ego thought system?

As for partners in relationships, the same principles and cautions apply. Over the years, we have heard many stories of couples who have broken up because one of the partners was not a Course student, *as if that external condition were a prerequisite for a happy life together.* The issue, naturally, is not that every couple should remain together, or that they should separate. However, using *A Course in Miracles* as an excuse for breaking up, or a reason for remaining together misses the whole point again. Very often, in fact, remaining with someone who is *not* a student of the Course may be the perfect classroom in which to learn that the heart of *A Course in Miracles* is its content of forgiveness, not the form in which that teaching comes. We shall return to this issue in the final chapter.

The same mistakes occur on the "other side" of relationships; i.e., the belief that students of the Course should not be involved in any romantic or sexual relationships at all, not to mention getting married and having children, since that would clearly reflect special relationships. However, it has been forgotten that specialness exists not in a relationship between *two people*, but in the *thoughts* of a person who has preferred the ego's individuality or specialness to the Holy Spirit's Love. The lack that inevitably follows such a decision must lead to seeking outside oneself for help in filling that lack, what the Course would describe as *the scarcity principle*. That filling up the perceived inner lack is what *A Course in Miracles* means by special relationships.

It is impossible to be born into this world *without* specialness, and it is simply denial that would lead students to believe that they are without this belief system. One of the core definitions the Course uses for specialness is substitution, and simply leaving Heaven—as all people in the world believe they have done—expresses the belief that the ego's specialness is a worthy and worthwhile substitute for the Love of God. Therefore, the special relationship is the rule of the separated world, and rather than deny it, students of *A Course in Miracles* should accept this perceptual fact, and turn to Jesus or the Holy Spirit for help in learning the lessons of forgiveness that this valuable classroom offers under Their guidance.

In other words, as we frequently remind students during our workshops and classes, when studying *A Course in Miracles*, students should above all *not* forget to be normal. And normal people serve on juries, become involved in litigation, carry insurance, get sick, become angry, laugh, cry, mourn the deaths of loved ones, have relationships, families, circles of friends, etc., etc., etc. The challenge is to be involved in all these normal human activities, but to do so differently— with Jesus instead of without him. Thus Jesus encourages his students to be like everyone else, but to be happy and peaceful:

> There is a way of living in the world that is not here, although it seems to be. *You do not change appearance, though you smile more frequently.* Your forehead is serene; your eyes are quiet (workbook, p. 284; W-pI.155.1:1-3; italics ours).

Therefore, as we cautioned in our discussion of the previous question, students of *A Course in Miracles* should watch for their ego's vigilance in judging other people's responses or behaviors, or their own for that matter. Jesus' loving judgment is always and only in terms of *content*—i.e., the inner teacher that is chosen—and never the *form*. And unless one has the egoless wisdom of the Holy Spirit, how can an observer possibly know which teacher has been chosen?

32) *A Course in Miracles* **teaches that anger is never justified. Does this mean I should never get angry, and that if I do, I am not being a good Course student or am not being spiritual enough?**

Jesus does in fact explicitly state in two places that anger (or attack) is never justified. In the introduction to his discussion of the crucifixion, he states:

> Anger always involves projection of separation, which must ultimately be accepted as one's own responsibility, rather than being blamed on others.... You cannot *be* attacked, attack *has* no justification, and you *are* responsible for what you believe (text, p. 84; T-6.in.1:2,7).

And later in the text, discussing why forgiveness is always justified, Jesus teaches:

> Anger is *never* justified. Attack has *no* foundation. It is here escape from fear begins, and will be made complete. Here is the real world given in exchange for dreams of terror.

For it is on this forgiveness rests, and is but natural (text, p. 593; T-30.VI.1:1-5).

Our answer here directly follows the discussion of the previous question, and goes to the heart of one's practice of *A Course in Miracles.* Jesus is not asking his students to be perfect; if they were, or even wanted to be, then they would have remained in Heaven—the only home of perfection—or would already have returned. The fact that students have need of *A Course in Miracles* is witnessing to their belief in the reality of imperfection. And imperfect people become angry and seek to avoid responsibility for their own choices. One can indeed say that the core thought of everyone's ego is to keep the individuality and specialness it believed it stole from God, but to avoid responsibility for it. Therefore, this avoidance can only occur by people blaming another for what they secretly believe *they* did, and thus attacking someone else for their sin.

Jesus' purpose in the Course is to help his students accept responsibility for their projections onto others. It would be most unrealistic of him to expect his students to have no attack thoughts, but it is a most reasonable goal to ask that students at least be aware of their egos' attempts to deny responsibility for being upset. Therefore, becoming angry does not mean one is not a good Course student, but becoming a "good" one means learning—or even being willing to learn—to be responsible for one's angry perceptions of others, and to be aware of one's own guilt over separation from the Love of God and the loving guidance of Jesus or the Holy Spirit. "Good" students thus would never seek to *justify* their angry thoughts or feelings; at the same time they would not be denying that they have them. This honesty allows Jesus or the Holy Spirit to help them change their minds, if they so choose. This is the gentle and loving way of understanding Jesus' statements in the text that we quoted above.

33) Is learning cumulative? That is, do I take what I have learned with me when I die, so that when I "come back" I do not have to begin all over again?

The premise of this question is that time is linear, and therefore one's learning can be measured within an evolving linear dimension. However, as we learn in *A Course in Miracles*, also discussed in the previous chapter, time is not linear since everything within the dream of time and space occurred within the original instant. And so learning does not really occur within the seemingly linear-based dream figure we call ourselves. Rather, our learning is simply the acceptance of the correction of forgiveness within our minds. This correction, held for us by the Holy Spirit, undoes—or unlearns—the ego's thought system of separation. It existed before the world of time and space was made, and it still remains in our minds. Our ability to choose this correction is also in our minds. And so it is what we have referred to as the decision maker—the part of our tri-partite minds that chooses—that *learns* the difference between the ego's lies and the Holy Spirit's truth. The physical and psychological self with which we identify, and which we believe does the learning, is simply the reflection in a world of time and space of the decision maker, whose choosing occurs outside the temporal and spatial dimensions.

This of course is not understandable to a brain that has been programmed to think only within the dimension of time and space, life and death. But we are assured by Jesus that our understanding is not necessary:

> You find it difficult to accept the idea that you need give so little, to receive so much. And it is very hard for you to realize it is not personally insulting that your contribution and the Holy Spirit's are so extremely disproportionate. You are still convinced that your understanding is a powerful contribution to the truth, and makes it what it is. Yet we have emphasized that you need understand nothing (text, p. 356; T-18.IV.7:3-6).

And so, even if we cannot truly understand how we learn the lessons of the Holy Spirit, we can at least understand how we do *not* learn them.

34) If all life here is an illusion, why does *A Course in Miracles* refer to "living things"?

Here again, we must understand Jesus' use of language. Passages in which that phrase appears, as in Lesson 195 for example, are written on the level of *our experience* and not Jesus' reality. For it is within the dream of our individual existence in this world that we indeed do form relationships with "living things." And therefore, as is the message of that lesson, we should feel grateful to those beings for the learning opportunities our relationships with them afford us; namely, that what we projected onto them is simply a mistaken belief in our own guilt.

For Jesus to insist that we relate to him on his level would indeed make no sense, as we have already discussed, for our experience remains rooted within the dream. And so his purpose of expressing his truth on the level of our capacity to understand must be recognized by Course students lest they seriously misinterpret his message. Jesus specifically tells us that there is no life outside Heaven, as we saw in an earlier question, and so there can be no "living things" in the world. But since we believe we are alive here, relating to other beings we believe are alive here as well, it would be pointless for Jesus to demand that we accept a truth that our fear precludes us from accepting at this time. Therefore, reflecting his gentle love for us, he speaks about "living things," even though on another level there is nothing living here at all.

35) *A Course in Miracles* teaches that all has already happened. Isn't this the same as *predestination*?

The traditional understanding of predestination, stemming from John Calvin, the 16th-century Protestant reformer, is that from the beginning of time God had chosen (predestined) those to be saved (the "elect") and those to be punished (the "sinners") in the future. And this decision was irrevocable and unchangeable.

The view of *A Course in Miracles* is that yes, everything has already happened—and in that sense the drama of the world is irrevocable ("the script is written")—but this includes *both* the ego's script and the Holy Spirit's correction for it. To re-quote an important passage:

> God gave His Teacher to replace the one you made.... And what He would replace has been replaced. Time lasted but an instant in your mind, with no effect upon eternity. And so is all time past, and everything exactly as it was before the way to nothingness was made. The tiny tick of time in which the first mistake was made, and all of them within that one mistake, held also the Correction for that one, and all of them that came within the first (text, p. 511; T-26.V.3:1-5).

Therefore, in *A Course in Miracles*, the agent of *predestination* is the decision maker, not God, for it is this aspect of the tri-partite or split mind that has authored the scripts of our lives in the physical universe. However, this same split mind has the capacity, through the decision maker, to choose at any given instant which teacher—the ego or Jesus—will guide us as we "review mentally" the scripts that have "already gone by." The "we," to make the point once again, is not the self we call ourselves by name, but rather the decision maker in our minds—outside time and space, and *outside* the ancient ego script. And here the choice is certainly not predestined. It is thus clear that the Course's statement "the script is written" is not to be understood temporally at all, while the traditional view of predestination is, for it is based upon a decision made by God in the past, which will inevitably be carried out in the future.

36) Is there such a thing as free will, and what is it anyway?

This question must be answered in two parts: 1) In *Heaven* there can be no free will, for how can the Son of God be free to choose when there is literally nothing there to choose from? In a non-dualistic reality, which *is* the state of Heaven, there is only perfect Oneness. That is why *A Course in Miracles* states that the Will of God and the will of His Son are one and the same. And so there can *be* nothing else, and therefore nothing to choose between. Moreover, the process of choosing has meaning only within a subject-object world: a subject who chooses among different objects, all perceived and experienced to be outside the mind that chooses. Therefore, the term *free will* has no meaning here, unless it is used as *A Course in Miracles* does in one place, to refer to the *freedom of will,* the title of a section in Chapter 30. However, in this instance the term means something quite different from the usual conception of *free will.* In Heaven, our will is free because it *cannot* be imprisoned, which is a statement that reflects the Atonement principle that the separation from God never happened. Therefore, the Son of God cannot truly be imprisoned by his own mistaken belief that he has sinned against his Creator, and thus been made a prisoner to his own guilt. We read in several places:

> How wonderful it is to do your will! For that is freedom. There is nothing else that ever should be called by freedom's name. Unless you do your will you are not free. And would God leave His Son without what he has chosen for himself? God but ensured that you would never lose your will when He gave you His perfect Answer. Hear It now, that you may be reminded of His Love and learn your will. God would not have His Son made prisoner to what he does not want. He joins with you in willing you be free. And to oppose Him is to make a choice against yourself, and choose that you be bound (text, p. 585; T-30.II.2).

> In the holy state the will is free, so that its creative power is unlimited and choice is meaningless (text, p. 70; T-5.II.6:4).

> It is not your will to be imprisoned because your will is free. That is why the ego is the denial of free will. It is never God Who coerces you, because He shares His Will with you. His Voice teaches only in accordance with His Will, but that is not the Holy Spirit's lesson because that is what you *are*. The lesson is that your will and God's cannot be out of accord because they are one (text, p. 130; T-8.II.3:2-6).

When we finally accept the Atonement for ourselves, awakening from the dream and thus becoming manifestations of the Holy Spirit, the recognition that our wills are one with God's must inevitably follow.

2) Within the *dream*, however, which is the realm of perception and illusion, the concept of free will becomes extremely important and meaningful for it is the mechanism of salvation. In his dream, the Son believed that he had chosen against God, and this set into motion the whole drama of the unholy trinity—sin, guilt, and fear—culminating in the making of the physical universe as a defense against the perceived wrathful vengeance of the ego's made-up God. Thus, within the dream, the same power of the Son's mind to choose *against* God, now must be free to choose *for* Him. And so Jesus states in a number of important passages:

> In this world the only remaining freedom is the freedom of choice; always between two choices or two voices. Will is not involved in perception at any level, and has nothing to do with choice (manual, p. 75; C-1.7:1-2).

> The power of his decision offers it to him as he requests. Herein lie hell and Heaven. The sleeping Son of God has but this power left to him (manual, p. 51; M-21.3:5-7).

> You have chosen to be in a state of opposition in which opposites are possible. As a result, there are choices you must make....Choosing depends on a split mind (text, p. 70; T-5.II.6:2-3,6).

Would you be hostage to the ego or host to God? You will accept only whom you invite. You are free to determine who shall be your guest, and how long he shall remain with you. *Yet this is not real freedom, for it still depends on how you see it (*text, p. 184; T-11.II.7:1-4; italics ours).

Indeed, one might say that a purpose of *A Course in Miracles* is for Jesus to teach us that we do have a choice within our dreams of separation and specialness, and that this choice rests within our minds. By learning the meaning of forgiveness, which is that our experience of the world is a projection of a decision in our minds that can now be changed, we learn to exercise this free will. Thus we ultimately learn and remember that our true will has been free all along. We simply had forgotten. And so Jesus states: "The Holy Spirit calls you both to remember [God] and to forget [the ego]" (text, p. 70; T-5.II.6:1).

37) How free are we in our everyday lives to act in our own best interests, especially if, as *A Course in Miracles* says, we are all hallucinating?

This answer begins where the previous one ends. Within the dream of our individual existence—the hallucination—we are free to choose. However, such choosing has nothing to do with what the world understands by choosing, especially when we think of trying to act in our own best interests. We *cannot* act in our best interests because, as the workbook reminds us, "I do not *perceive* my own best interests" (workbook, p. 36-37; W-pI.24; italics ours). This is a crucial aspect in the understanding of the Course, and the above lesson states the point clearly:

In no situation that arises do you realize the outcome that would make you happy. Therefore, you have no guide to appropriate action, and no way of judging the result. What you do is determined by your perception of the situation, and that perception is wrong. It is inevitable, then, that you will not serve your own best interests. Yet they are your only goal in any situation which is correctly perceived. Otherwise, you will not recognize what they are.

If you realized that you do not perceive your own best interests, you could be taught what they are. But in the presence of your conviction that you do know what they are, you cannot learn (workbook, p. 36; W-pI.24.1:1–2:2).

Therefore, throughout *A Course in Miracles*, Jesus urges us to consult either him or the Holy Spirit, for They are the only ones Who *do* know what our best interests are. And these, naturally, always involve the change of mind or perception that reflects our decisions to forgive instead of to attack. On our own, we cannot forgive, let alone know what choices we should make. However, we are always free to choose our teacher, and in that choice we have *already* acted in our own best interests. And this, and only this, is the meaning of free will within this world of illusion, for it is from the right mind alone that the right choice—our best interest—can result. Thus it is that Jesus addresses his students: "Resign now as your own teacher…for you were badly taught" (text, pp. 211,548; T-12.V.8:3; T-28.I.7:1), and he asks that they choose instead the Teacher Whose wisdom will always teach them correctly.

38) *A Course in Miracles* **says that there is no love without ambivalence. Does this mean that I never come from a loving space, and that all my thoughts and actions are from my ego?**

No, it certainly does not. The specific statement in the Course is as follows:

> You project onto the ego the decision to separate, and this conflicts with the love you feel for the ego because you made it. No love in this world is without this ambivalence, and since no ego has experienced love without ambivalence the concept is beyond its understanding. Love will enter

immediately into any mind that truly wants it, but it must want it truly. This means that it wants it without ambivalence, and this kind of wanting is wholly without the ego's "drive to get" (text, p. 55; T-4.III.4:5-8).

This passage clearly implies that when we choose the correction of the Holy Spirit in our right minds—the holy instant—and truly let go of our egos, we can become a reflection of love, a manifestation of the Holy Spirit. In this case, it is indeed possible to come from a loving space. In fact, the principal goal of the Course is to have students learn to access their right minds, the loving home of the Holy Spirit. However, one needs to be discerning, for very often the ego's special love can appear to be identical to the Holy Spirit's real Love. The ego's unconscious "drive to get"—the core of specialness—is still very much present, and serves to mask the truth with the clever lies of illusion.

Any thought, word, or deed that proceeds from the wrong mind, even though it *appears as loving*, cannot be so. Therefore, to evaluate any interaction by appearances can be but a lack of discernment stemming from our need to appear loving and understanding; in other words, what our egos would bless as "spiritually enlightened" behavior. We should not underestimate the need each one of us has to be accepted by others because we want to be judged by them as loving. This need becomes a powerful interference to choosing our right minds, wherein lies the only real love.

Sometimes the most loving action, emanating from our right minds, would be to say "No" to someone's request, incurring their disappointment and anger. That is why Jesus states:

> To learn this course requires willingness to question every value that you hold. Not one can be kept hidden and obscure but it will jeopardize your learning. No belief is neutral. Every one has the power to dictate each decision you make (text, p. 464; T-24.in.2:1-4).

Let us suppose that an unconscious *value* that our egos hold is to be popular and admired by many for being a loving and thoughtful person. Our whole life's script then, emanating from our wrong minds, revolves around being this kind of dream figure. We might achieve our goal, but at what cost? Students of *A Course in Miracles* sometimes make this mistake of judging by appearance and form. Sometimes the most difficult correction for us to accept is to go against some "cherished value" of our egos—above all, the models of special love and special hate relationships. If students can be reasonably clear that they have uncovered their unconscious ego values and have the little willingness to access the correction in their right minds—getting themselves out of the way—then they will be manifestations of the thought system of the Holy Spirit and not the ego.

Indeed, our daily practice of forgiveness is what allows us to be increasingly in touch with this loving Presence of truth in our split minds, so that our thoughts, words, and deeds can express this truth. Therefore, it is certainly possible that our lives can come from our right minds and not our wrong minds, from the Holy Spirit and not the ego. It is this process of increasingly reflecting love instead of hate that brings us to the gate of Heaven, beyond which *is* the Love of God.

39) What is the role of meditation in practicing *A Course in Miracles*?

Meditation as such is not an integral part of the Course's curriculum. Certainly one can take the workbook lessons and their one-year training program to be exercises in meditation. But, again, these are only meant for a one-year period. However, Jesus would never object to his students spending quiet time with him, asking for help in removing the blocks of guilt and hate that interfere with their awareness of his loving presence. Nevertheless, he specifically cautions students not to make idols of their regular periods of spiritual practice, even

though they may still require structure, part of which, naturally, could be times of meditation or quiet:

> But what about those who have not reached his [an
> advanced teacher of God's] certainty? They are not yet ready
> for such lack of structuring on their own part. What must they
> do to learn to give the day to God? There are some general
> rules which do apply, although each one must use them as
> best he can in his own way. *Routines as such are dangerous,
> because they easily become gods in their own right, threaten-
> ing the very goals for which they were set up* (manual, p. 38;
> M-16.2:1-5; italics ours).

In "I Need Do Nothing," originally a special message to
Helen, Jesus specifically discusses how his Course is *not* a
course in meditation, but rather has a much different focus.
This does not make it necessarily better than other paths, but
it does establish how different it is from them:

> Many have spent a lifetime in preparation, and have indeed
> achieved their instants of success. This course does not
> attempt to teach more than they learned in time, but it does
> aim at saving time.... It is extremely difficult to reach Atone-
> ment by fighting against sin. Enormous effort is expended in
> the attempt to make holy what is hated and despised [the
> body]. *Nor is a lifetime of contemplation and long periods of
> meditation aimed at detachment from the body necessary.* All
> such attempts will ultimately succeed because of their pur-
> pose. Yet the means are tedious and very time consuming, for
> all of them look to the future for release from a state of present
> unworthiness and inadequacy.
> Your way will be different, not in purpose but in means.
> ... You are not making use of the course if you insist on using
> means which have served others well, neglecting what was
> made for *you* (text, p. 362-63; T-18.VII.4:4-5,7-11; 5:1; 6:5;
> italics ours in 4:9).

And so, students of *A Course in Miracles* would be silly *not*
to meditate, if such a practice is beneficial to their spiritual
path. And Jesus, again, would hardly seek to dissuade them.

However, he would caution them, as we have seen, *not* to make the meditative practice a source of dependency. It should be a means, not an end. Moreover, it would certainly be a mistake if such students felt that *all* students of *A Course in Miracles* must meditate, simply because they did. Students should never forget that the curriculum is highly individualized, and that the personal curriculum is undertaken between each individual student and the Holy Spirit.

There is another caution we may note here regarding dependency and meditation. The clear purpose of *A Course in Miracles*, and specifically the workbook, is for its students to generalize the lessons and principles to *all* aspects of their daily lives, at *all* times. It would be directly against this purpose to have students *need* to take time out from a difficult situation so as to go apart and be externally quiet. This clearly would never work in the midst of a traffic jam, a difficult meeting, a psychotherapy session, a classroom, a car filled with boisterous children, etc. If the quiet cannot be internalized so that one knows that Jesus or the Holy Spirit is always present in the mind, then the actual meditation has been of little use. Rather, students should aim at generalizing these quiet times to *all* times, learning how accessible their true Teacher is.

40) What is the "holy instant," and what is its role in the Atonement?

In a sense, understanding the holy instant parallels understanding the question of meditation we discussed above. The holy instant is not a period of meditation wherein the student has a "good experience," and feels the presence of Jesus or the Holy Spirit. On the contrary, the holy instant is the Course's term for the *instant*—outside time and space—when we choose the Holy Spirit as our teacher instead of the ego. It is the correction of forgiveness for the ego's "unholy instant" of judgment and attack, the experience of *un*doing our guilt through Jesus' help. It is this purpose which makes the instant holy, and establishes it as an integral part of the overall Atonement plan for correcting our misperceptions and misthoughts.

Moreover, the holy instant can be understood as the steps we take throughout our lives that gradually lead us closer and closer to the real world, in a sense the ultimate holy instant. Each time we are tempted to listen to the ego's tale of specialness and the need for attack, we are reminded by Jesus that we can choose a miracle instead—"Let miracles replace all grievances" (workbook, pp. 137-38; W-pI.78)—and have him help us make the shift in perception that constitutes the essence of forgiveness, the heart of the holy instant. In other words, the holy instants are the "little steps" of forgiveness the Course refers to that are the means for helping us undo our illusions so that we may reach our goal of truth. As we read in the Course:

> Against the ego's insane notion of salvation the Holy Spirit gently lays the holy instant.... The holy instant is the opposite of the ego's fixed belief in salvation through vengeance for the past.... In the holy instant the power of the Holy Spirit will prevail, because you joined Him.... Release your brothers from the slavery of their illusions by forgiving them for the illusions you perceive in them. Thus will you learn that you have been forgiven, for it is you who offered them illusions. In the holy instant this is done for you in time, to bring you the true condition of Heaven (text, pp. 324-25; T-16.VII.6:1,3; 7:3; 9:5-7).

41) What does *A Course in Miracles* mean by "releasing your brother"? How can I save him if the world is an hallucination in my mind?

The reader should recall our earlier discussion in question 5 of Jesus' use of metaphor in the Course. In other words, students of *A Course in Miracles* need to allow themselves to be led beyond the *form* of its words to their underlying *content*. This is a process that occurs slowly over time, beginning with a more literal understanding of the Course's teachings. At first, therefore, phrases like "releasing your brother," or parallel ones about being your brother's savior, or the workbook emphasis on being the light of the world, help students undo their negative self-image such as is summarized in workbook Lesson 93:

> You think you are the home of evil, darkness and sin. You think if anyone could see the truth about you he would be repelled, recoiling from you as if from a poisonous snake. You think if what is true about you were revealed to you, you would be struck with horror so intense that you would rush to death by your own hand, living on after seeing this being impossible (workbook, p. 159; W-pI.93.1).

It is a healing correction to be told that our thoughts about ourselves are not true, and that not only are we loved by God as an extension of His Will (as the rest of the lesson makes clear) but that we have the power to heal and bless others as well. It is only as we progress in our work with *A Course in Miracles* that it becomes clear that the process of "releasing" one's brother has nothing to do with our brother, but everything to do with ourselves. Indeed, this process of forgiveness can have nothing to do with our brother because in truth it is our dream, and he is but a figure in this dream. In one rather strong passage, Jesus asks his students:

> What if you recognized this world is an hallucination? What if you really understood you made it up? What if you realized that those who seem to walk about in it, to sin and die, attack and murder and destroy themselves, are wholly unreal? (text, p. 413; T-20.VIII.7:3-5)

In other words, our world and lives are our dreams, just as our sleeping dreams—with all their figures and events—are present only in our dreaming minds that in a sense are but hallucinations, too. Moreover, since the content of the ego's dream is fear, hate, victimization, and unforgiveness, all dream figures will have the above themes scripted throughout the dreaming we call "life." Therefore, there is no one to forgive because, again, all the people in our lives are simply made-up figures in our dreams. Who needs to be forgiven is ourselves—for dreaming in the first place instead of remembering our Identity as Christ, awake in God.

Our function of "releasing our brothers" through forgiveness relates to a function and process that truly occurs only within our minds—the home of dreams—although it is experienced by us as occurring between two separated individuals. By choosing Jesus as our teacher instead of the ego, by listening to his voice of forgiveness instead of the ego's voice of attack, we join with him as expressions of the Alternative that is in everyone's mind. And thus we become the reminders to our brothers that they can make the same choice we did, and thus be released from their guilt since we both scripted each other into our respective dreams. Therefore, we can choose either to be symbols of guilt or forgiveness for one another. This process of healing through forgiveness is summarized in this wonderfully clear passage from the manual for teachers, which discusses the role of the teacher of God when confronted by sickness:

> To them [the sick] God's teachers come, to represent another choice which they had forgotten. The simple presence of a teacher of God is a reminder.... They stand for the Alternative. With God's Word in their minds they come in benediction, not to heal the sick but to remind them of the remedy God has already given them.... Very gently they call to their brothers to turn away from death: "Behold, you Son of God, what Life can offer you. Would you choose sickness in place of this?" (manual, p. 18; M-5.III.2:1-2,6-7,11-12)

Therefore, we save the world and everyone in it by saving or changing our *thoughts* about the world. By releasing ourselves from our own guilt, we release the world because we are one with it, since it is our projection. That is what the Course means by saying that we "arose with him [Jesus] when he began to save the world" (manual, p. 86; C-6.5:5). Our minds are one, and Jesus' remaining one with the Holy Spirit becomes the shining reminder in the Sonship's mind to do the same. Our making that choice allows us to be Jesus' manifestation to our brothers, just as he is the Holy Spirit's manifestation for us all (manual, p. 86; C-6.5:1-2). It is this call to remember and to choose that is the true release that heals.

42) What does *A Course in Miracles* mean by *forgiving your brother*? What if he does not accept the forgiveness, or is no longer physically present? Does this mean I can no longer forgive him?

Our answer is a continuation of the answer to the previous question. We are asked in the Course to forgive others for what they have *not* done to us. This is understood only by remembering that there is in truth no one out there to forgive. What we really forgive (or release) are the projections of guilt we have placed upon figures in our dreams that we scripted to be our special love or special hate partners. Therefore, it does not matter if these persons are physically present, know us personally, or even if they have already died. They continue to be present in our minds through our unforgiving thoughts, and the opportunity to ask for help to forgive these thoughts and projected images always remains.

The effects of our forgiveness are also fully present in our minds, joined with the minds of others. If other people choose not to accept our forgiveness in their dreams, the healed thought in our minds is no less efficacious. As the Course teaches, the Holy Spirit holds this forgiveness in the minds of the others until they are ready to accept it. That is the process Jesus is referring to as well when he says to us in the Course:

> I have saved all your kindnesses and every loving thought you ever had. I have purified them of the errors that hid their light, and kept them for you in their own perfect radiance.

They are beyond destruction and beyond guilt (text, p. 76; T-5.IV.8:3-5).

Likewise, he saves our loving thoughts towards others, and holds them until they are ready to accept them for themselves.

43) How does one tell the difference between the Holy Spirit and the ego?

We begin with a statement from the Course. It comes in "The Test of Truth" in Chapter 14 of the text, and is the answer to this question, given in the context of discerning between the "dark lessons" of the ego and the "bright lessons" of the Holy Spirit:

> You have one test, as sure as God, by which to recognize if what you learned is true. [1] If you are wholly free of fear of any kind, and [2] if all those who meet or even think of you share in your perfect peace, then you can be sure that you have learned God's lesson, and not your own (text, p. 276; T-14.XI.5:1-2).

In other words, Jesus is providing his students with two criteria with which to evaluate whether they have chosen the ego or himself as their teacher. The first deals only with individual students, whether or not they are at peace. The second involves other people, those who live and work with us, not to mention everyone else. We all would have to admit that it is relatively simple to delude ourselves into thinking we have chosen the Holy Spirit, when in truth we have chosen our own specialness. But it is more difficult to fool other people, especially those who know us well and who see us regularly over periods of time. Incidentally, students of *A Course in Miracles* sometimes wonder if that second criterion would have to exclude Jesus, since obviously the biblical figure (who, by the way, should *never* be taken for the historical Jesus—see question 52 on page 102 below) was crucified by angry people who quite clearly did not "share in [his] perfect peace." However, one should understand this situation to mean that people may experience your perfect peace, but may be so threatened by it that they try to attack it and you. But they could not be doing so had they not first experienced this peace as authentic, and *then* become threatened by it.

This test of truth is applicable to students over the long run because, again, it is difficult to fool others and even oneself over a period of time. However, in any given instant when one wishes to know which teacher has been consulted, it is almost impossible to know for certain. As all students of *A Course in Miracles* already know, and as we have already commented, the ego can quite deceptively pose like the Holy Spirit. Given the tremendous investment all people in this world have in maintaining their specialness, it should come as no surprise that this would be so. In this very important passage, Jesus cautions his students about underestimating the power their specialness has to mask the Holy Spirit's Voice. It is from one of the major sections in the text that deals specifically with the treacherous nature of specialness:

> You are not special. If you think you are, and would defend your specialness against the truth of what you really are, how can you know the truth? What answer that the Holy Spirit gives can reach you, when it is your specialness to which you listen, and which asks and answers. Its tiny answer, soundless in the melody that pours from God to you eternally in loving praise of what you are, is all you listen to. And that vast song of honor and of love for what you are seems silent and unheard before its "mightiness." You strain your ears to hear its soundless voice, *and yet the Call of God Himself is soundless to you.*
>
> *You can defend your specialness, but never will you hear the Voice for God beside it* (text, p. 467; T-24.II.4:1–5:1; italics ours).

Therefore, our response to this question is to state, that because of students' over-identification with their egos, it is really the wrong question to ask. Rather, the focus should be on eliminating the *interference* to hearing the Holy Spirit's Voice, which would then simply allow the Voice for God to be Itself. Thus, the question should be: "Why don't I practice the forgiveness lessons the Holy Spirit asks me to do so that I can better hear His Voice?" With this new question, the focus is now shifted to eliminating the problem so that the Answer can be given us. As Jesus exhorts his students:

> Your task is not to seek for love [or hear the Holy Spirit's Voice], but merely to seek and find all of the barriers within yourself that you have built against it. It is not necessary to seek for what is true, but it *is* necessary to seek for what is false (text, p. 315; T-16.IV.6:1-2).

And returning to "The Test of Truth," we find Jesus making the same point to his students who despair over being able to actually hear the Holy Spirit, given the strength of their investment in their ego's "dark lessons":

> Do not be concerned about how you can learn a lesson so completely different from everything that you have taught yourself. How would you know? Your part is very simple. You need only recognize that everything you learned you do not want. Ask to be taught, and do not use your experiences to confirm what you have learned. When your peace is threatened or disturbed in any way, say to yourself:
>
> *I do not know what anything, including this, means. And so I do not know how to respond to it. And I will not use my own past learning as the light to guide me now.*
>
> By this refusal to attempt to teach yourself what you do not know, the Guide Whom God has given you will speak to you. He will take His rightful place in your awareness the instant you abandon it, and offer it to Him (text, pp. 276-77; T-14.XI.6).

The primary focus of Jesus' Course is always on removing the interferences to the awareness of love's presence (text, intro.; T-in.1:7), *and not on the love itself.* And so, once again, the students' focus will remain on asking Jesus' help to set aside their ego thought system, rather than on asking him directly for help or guidance with things in the world. Finally, we cite one important passage in the text that underscores this major emphasis:

> The task of the miracle worker... becomes *to deny the denial of truth* (text, p. 203; T-12.II.1:5).

The "denial of truth" is of course the ego thought system, which denies the truth of God. Our responsibility is to ask the Holy Spirit's help to "deny" the validity of what the ego teaches, hereby affirming His truth of the Atonement.

44) Is it a bad sign if I do not "hear" an inner Voice? Does that mean that I am not being a good student of *A Course in Miracles*?

In actuality, within the dream there are literally two "inner voices"—one of the wrong mind (the ego) and that of the right mind (the Holy Spirit), and the differences between them, as we have already seen, cannot be as easily discerned as students might hope and believe. In order to maintain its individuality and uniqueness, each member of the Sonship has listened to the ego's voice and followed its plan. A cursory view of the history of this planet, along with its current affairs, will testify and witness heavily to such a fact.

Indeed, it is *not* the easiest thing in the world to be able to "hear" the Voice for God, the Course's term for the Holy Spirit. In fact, *A Course in Miracles* itself says that "very few can hear God's Voice at all, and even they cannot communicate His messages directly through the Spirit which gave them" (manual, p. 30; M-12.3:3). Our investments in specialness and the need to maintain our individuality, *almost always unconscious*, make it very difficult to hear the Voice that speaks for the undoing of specialness. In the previous question, we quoted a passage that explicitly addresses this problem. All too often, sincere students of *A Course in Miracles* are convinced that they are hearing the Voice of the Holy Spirit, when all they are really listening to is their own egos extolling their specialness and uniqueness, within the framework of what they *want* to believe is a special mission.

Another source of misunderstanding for many students of *A Course in Miracles* is the specific Identity of the Holy Spirit's Voice. One does not fail the Course if a "Voice" is not heard internally as Helen heard. Furthermore, we should not try to limit how and in which way the Holy Spirit can reach us. For example, a dream at night, a conversation with a friend, an intuitive thought, a book we read, a class we take—can all be used by the Holy Spirit to present us with a correction for our wrong-minded thinking.

In conclusion, to restate this important point, we can say that the only criterion for being a "good" Course student is having the little willingness to learn the Holy Spirit's lessons of undoing our egos through forgiveness. Specifically *hearing* an inner voice—again, as did Helen—can therefore be understood as irrelevant in this context.

45) Do Jesus or the Holy Spirit send me my lessons?

No, they do not. Here again, we see an example of students taking the words of *A Course in Miracles* literally, the result being that conclusions are drawn that are the exact opposite of what Jesus is actually teaching in his Course. To be sure, there are passages with words stating that the Holy Spirit (or Jesus) provide lessons for us, send people to us, or that we are sent to others. However, it is essential that students of *A Course in Miracles*, if they are to grow in their learning and practice of its principles, understand that statements such as these— clearly in the minority when taken against the whole of the Course's teaching—are meant to reach those who are basically just beginning their spiritual journey with the Course. And so Jesus couches his teachings in words that his students—always referred to as children (or sometimes even younger)—can understand without fear.

Our *experience* is that we are very much a part of this physical world, just as we believe God is. There is, for example, this very important line in the text, which we have already quoted: "You cannot even think of God without a body, or in some form you think you recognize" (text, p. 364; T-18.VIII.1:7). Therefore, as we discussed earlier in question 5, it would not be helpful nor practical for Jesus to impose a level of explanation beyond his students' capacity to understand. As he states so clearly in the workbook: "For who can understand a language far beyond his simple grasp?" (workbook, p. 355; W-pI.192.2:2). Thus, we can recognize again that Jesus uses language to serve as a bridge from the level of his students' experience to his truth.

In fact, the Holy Spirit or Jesus do nothing in the world, because all correction and healing occur at the level of the mind. "There is no world!" as Jesus states emphatically in the workbook: "This is the central thought the course attempts to teach" (workbook, p. 237; W-pI.132.6:2-3). Jesus' presence exists only in our *minds*, since that is all there is. Ideas leave not their source, and so the dream has never left the mind of the dreamer, however compellingly real the world appears to be to us. This is similar to the experience everyone has when asleep at night and dreaming. While asleep, the dreamer actually believes that the activities occurring in the dream are quite real, and reacts accordingly with feelings of happiness, fear, joy, or anxiety, not to mention physical concomitants as well, such as tachycardia, excessive perspiration, etc. However, upon waking, the dreamer realizes that "it was only a dream." Similar to what we discussed above in question 22 on page 38, we understand that nothing has occurred other than within the mind of the dreamer, which contained the various images and symbols that *seemed* to be so real. As Jesus repeatedly points out in the Course, there is no difference whatsoever between our sleeping and waking experiences. They are both simply dreams occurring within the larger dream of separation. As he says in the text:

> *All* your time is spent in dreaming. Your sleeping and your waking dreams have different forms, and that is all. Their content is the same. They are your protest against reality, and your fixed and insane idea that you can change it. In your waking dreams, the special relationship has a special place. It is the means by which you try to make your sleeping dreams come true (text, p. 351; T-18.II.5:12-17; italics ours).

And so it would make no sense for our wise inner teacher, Jesus, to fall into the same trap that the world does, of making the error real by seeing problems existing there, and therefore their solutions as well. However, as long as we believe that we are here, with problems and answers here, our *experience* will be that our help will be here, too. The loving presence of Jesus in our right minds—a mind which we have denied—will inevitably be experienced in the body and the world, *even though he is not there*. Participating in the process of forgiveness, students of *A Course in Miracles* gradually realize that they are the dreamers and not the dream, and that their existence is in the mind and not the body. Eventually, the realization also occurs that Jesus or the Holy Spirit is only within their minds.

And what is Their function within the mind? To restate what we discussed previously, Their function is simply to remind the Son of God that he has made a faulty choice (by choosing the ego as his teacher), and now can make the correct one. His attention, via the miracle, has been restored to his mind, where the wrong decision was made and the presence of the Holy Spirit reminds him he can choose again. Early in the text, Jesus describes the functioning of the Holy Spirit this way:

> The Voice of the Holy Spirit does not command, because It is incapable of arrogance. It does not demand, because It does not seek control. It does not overcome, because It does not attack. It merely reminds. It is compelling only because of

what It reminds you *of*. It brings to your mind the other way, remaining quiet even in the midst of the turmoil you may make (text, p. 70; T-5.II.7:1-6).

And so *we*—the decision maker in our minds—are the ones who write and choose our scripts, and the role of Jesus is to *remind* us that we can make another choice in how we look at what we have chosen. That looking with his love beside us is the core of the Course's meaning of forgiveness. We are the ones who chose wrongly, and therefore we are the ones who must choose differently, as Jesus exhorts us at the end of the text:

> Trials are but lessons that you failed to learn presented once again, so where you made a faulty choice before you now can make a better one, and thus escape all pain that what you chose before has brought to you. In every difficulty, all distress, and each perplexity Christ calls to you and gently says, "My brother, choose again" (text, p. 620; T-31.VIII. 3:1-2).

Again, we are the ones who present ourselves with our scripts, and it is our minds that choose whether to have our egos or Jesus be the teacher guiding us through these experiences.

Therefore, it is not the Holy Spirit that *brings* us parking spaces, *sends* certain people to be helped by us or for us to be helped by, or *causes* us to be raped as a forgiveness lesson, as one poor student of *A Course in Miracles* believed about a very painful experience in her own life. Such mistaken thoughts about the Holy Spirit, besides having potentially tragic implications, help students to avoid responsibility for their own choices by transferring them over to the Holy Spirit or Jesus. And then they justify such misperceptions by quoting—out of context!—passages from the Course to support their positions of specialness.

And so it is extremely important, to make this point still once again, for students of *A Course in Miracles* not to confuse the *form* of the Course's teaching with its underlying

content. Otherwise growth will not occur, and they would forever remain at the lower levels of their journey up the spiritual
ladder that the Course provides. Therefore, the purpose for
students being told that the Holy Spirit does things for them in
the world, is to be healed of the ego's basic thought system
that teaches that there *is* no Holy Spirit, and even if there were,
He certainly would not be a friendly Presence which would
comfort and guide them. Thus, it is not the words (the *form*)
that are the true teaching of the Course, but their underlying
meaning (the *content*). Jesus' purpose in using this metaphoric
language is to help his students undo the ego thoughts that a
wrathful and avenging God will punish them for their sin.

Once the belief is corrected that God (or the Holy Spirit or
Jesus) is our enemy, we are able to advance along to the next
steps of our journey. These include the increasing recognition,
as we approach the journey's end, of the essentially abstract
reality of the Holy Spirit's and Jesus' presence in our split
minds. What is at issue here is the crucial point of proceeding
slowly and patiently along the spiritual path, minimizing the
inevitable fear of eventually letting go of one's individual
identity. As Jesus so gently comforts us, using the metaphor of
dreams:

> The Holy Spirit, ever practical in His wisdom, accepts
> your dreams and uses them as means for waking. You would
> have used them to remain asleep. I said before that the first
> change, before dreams disappear, is that your dreams of fear
> are changed to happy dreams. That is what the Holy Spirit
> does in the special relationship. He does not destroy it, nor
> snatch it away from you. But He does use it differently, as a
> help to make His purpose real to you. The special relationship
> will remain, not as a source of pain and guilt, but as a source
> of joy and freedom.... In your relationship the Holy Spirit has
> gently laid the real world; the world of happy dreams, from
> which awaking is so easy and so natural (text, pp. 351-52;
> T-18.II.6:1-7; 9:4).

Thus students are not asked to progress directly from the illusory nightmares of special relationships to the reality of the one relationship with God, but with Jesus as their guide, they first pass through the illusory dreams of forgiveness. These happy dreams undo the ego interference, which then allows the Love of God to return to their awareness. Therefore, as students of *A Course in Miracles*, they first learn that God is a loving Father rather than a hateful one, and the Holy Spirit a comforting companion to them in the world rather than their enemy. *Only then* can they learn that there is in fact no world for Them to comfort us *in*. Metaphor has served its purpose, and now can give way to the simple truth of the Oneness in God that lies beyond all words, and which is the ultimate goal of *A Course in Miracles*.

46) If God does not even know about us or the world, what is the meaning or purpose of prayer?

Prayer in the traditional sense has no place in the theory or practice of *A Course in Miracles*. For most formal religions, prayer implores a God perceived to be outside oneself to intercede, intervene, or otherwise be involved in a perceived problem affecting oneself or others. The problem is thus always seen as being outside the mind, and outside the person's ability to solve. And God, in the sense seen in the classical Greek plays, is perceived as the *deus ex machina* (literally meaning "God out of the machine") who suddenly and quite magically enters into our world to fix what has gone awry, just as was done in the performances of the ancient plays when an actual machine appeared on stage carrying the god who made all things right at the end. If God were to operate in this way (including of course Jesus or the Holy Spirit, His representatives in the dream), then He would be violating the Course's "prime directive" (to borrow a term from *Star Trek*), which is not to make the error real (text, p. 157; T-9.IV.4:1-6; "The Song of Prayer" p. 9; S-2.I.3:3-4), which trying to fix an illusory problem in an illusory world would certainly do.

That is why Jesus states early in the text that "the only meaningful prayer is for forgiveness, because those who have been forgiven have everything" (text, p. 40; T-3.V.6:3). And of course asking for help of the Holy Spirit to access our right minds is a form of this prayer. Forgiveness undoes the mind's misthought that there actually is a problem that has to be resolved. The real problem, naturally, is the *belief* that there is a problem in the first place. And so we need not pray for an external figure to remove an external problem. Rather, we pray for help in reminding ourselves that indeed there is only one problem (the belief in separation) and one solution (Atonement), and moreover, this problem has *already* been solved (workbook, pp. 139-42; W-pI.79,80). The answer but waits for our acceptance.

For a more complete treatment of the subject of prayer, the reader is referred to the scribed pamphlet, "The Song of Prayer," specifically, the first section called "Prayer."

47) It seems as if things are becoming worse since I began working with *A Course in Miracles*. Is this common? Am I doing something wrong?

While it is always difficult to respond to students' individual experiences without knowing much more about them, there are still some general observations we can make. It is indeed the case that with many students of *A Course in Miracles*, their work with it seems to intensify ego conflicts rather than alleviate them. In fact, what is often occurring is that ego thoughts which had been kept denied for so long are now being raised to awareness—an example of the important Course principle of bringing illusion to the truth, or darkness to the light—so that they can be looked at with Jesus or the Holy Spirit, and thus let go. Since it is fear that keeps our guilt denied, raising this guilt to awareness—always expressed in some aspect of specialness—will inevitably lead to an experience of fear. This is what is meant by these two powerful statements in the text that specifically address this experience. The first relates to our choosing Jesus as our guide instead of the ego, and the ego's angry response to such perceived treachery:

> Would you know the Will of God for you? Ask it of me who know it for you and you will find it. I will deny you nothing, as God denies me nothing. Ours is simply the journey back to God Who is our home. Whenever fear intrudes anywhere along the road to peace, it is because the ego has attempted to join the journey with us and cannot do so. *Sensing defeat and angered by it, the ego regards itself as rejected and becomes retaliative* (text, p. 137; T-8.V.5:1-6; italics ours).

The second passage, from the section "The Two Evaluations," explains the ego's reaction when we choose the Holy Spirit's loving evaluation of ourselves, rather than the ego's unloving one:

> You, then, have two conflicting evaluations of yourself in your mind, and they cannot both be true. You do not yet realize how completely different these evaluations are, because you do not understand how lofty the Holy Spirit's perception of you really is. He is not deceived by anything you do, because He never forgets what you are. The ego is deceived by everything you do, especially when you respond to the Holy Spirit, because at such times its confusion increases. *The ego is, therefore, particularly likely to attack you when you react lovingly, because it has evaluated you as unloving and you are going against its judgment. The ego will attack your motives as soon as they become clearly out of accord with its perception of you. This is when it will shift abruptly from suspiciousness to viciousness, since its uncertainty is increased* (text, p. 164; T-9.VII.4:1-7; italics ours).

Both of these passages must not be understood literally in the sense that the ego actually *believes* and *feels* these things that are attributed to it. Jesus anthropomorphizes the ego in the

Course so that it will be easier for his students to understand its dynamics. As he explains early in the text:

> I have spoken of the ego as if it were a separate thing, acting on its own. This was necessary to persuade you that you cannot dismiss it lightly, and must realize how much of your thinking is ego-directed (text, p. 61; T-4.VI.1:3-4).

The ego's "retaliation" and "viciousness" are simply metaphors to describe students' fear when confronted by the threat to their own special and individual identities. The loving presence of Jesus within our dream, reflecting the Holy Spirit's evaluation of us, represents the core of this threat to the ego's thought system. This fear is what leads to the defense of projection, which must take the form either of behaving or thinking viciously towards another (anger), or towards oneself (sickness). It is these "ego attacks" of anger or pain that lead to the perception and experience that "things are becoming worse."

In summary, then, we can frequently see that these difficult periods—referred to in the manual for teachers as "periods of unsettling"—can be "good signs"; i.e., that students are actually progressing in their journey of forgiveness with the Course. However, this by no means should be taken to mean that this is *always* the case. Students must learn to discern these "positive" signs from the "negative" ones where they may be plunging further into the ego's hell, and would then need some external help. Those students, in particular, who place themselves in the role of teacher or therapist of *A Course in Miracles* and have no training or supervised experience in these areas have to be vigilant against their own specialness needs interfering with the application of sound judgment in circumstances where another is in serious trouble and in deep need of help. Unfortunately, over a period of many years we have observed many painful and tragic consequences of untrained people serving as counselors and therapists for others who were in serious emotional difficulty. Their intervention sometimes exacerbated the problem rather than alleviating it, even to the point of precipitating breakdowns that required hospitalization.

48) If I practice *A Course in Miracles* faithfully, will I disappear?

This is a very commonly expressed concern of Course students, and reflects the same confusion of levels that we have commented on earlier. Level One, which is our term for the Course's metaphysical foundation, is uncompromising in seeing no reconciliation between truth and illusion, eternity and time. On this level, it takes no time to return to the formlessness of Heaven because we have never left it. To recall this important and previously quoted line: "You are at home in God, dreaming of exile." Our "journey without a distance" (text, p. 139; T-8.VI.9:7) requires no time to complete. On Level Two, however, which reflects our temporal experience within the dream, our journey home takes as long as we require. In fact, early in the text, Jesus observes that the collective end of the dream will occur over "millions" of years (text, p. 30; T-2.VIII.2:5), certainly suggesting that he is aware of the need to undo the Son's fear slowly and gently. Indeed, as we have already seen, many, many passages in *A Course in Miracles* reflect this awareness. Therefore, students should take comfort in a line like the following, which indicates that their fears of disappearing "into the Heart of God" are groundless:

> Fear not that you will be abruptly lifted up and hurled into reality (text, p. 322; T-16.VI.8:1).

The process of growth that is fostered by *A Course in Miracles* is always a gradual one, under the gentle and patient guidance of Jesus or the Holy Spirit. Using his own words, we can speak of a "slowly evolving training program," which is a "fairly slow process" (manual, p. 25; M-9.1:7; 2:4). Students of *A Course in Miracles* should beware of those who counsel them to "speed-up" this process of forgiveness. While on the larger level the spirituality of *A Course in Miracles* does save time, as Jesus repeatedly emphasizes, there is a quite different emphasis on the level of individual experience. There, students must proceed slowly and gently, otherwise, as indicated above, they will precipitate a panic attack. This same concern on Jesus' part is expressed at the very end of Chapter 1 in the text where he urges his students to prepare themselves for the later parts of their journey, so that they will not become "too fearful" and their experiences "traumatic."

And so, students of *A Course in Miracles* need not be afraid of losing their identity or individuality. As they progress in their study and practice of the Course, what they will lose will be their guilt, anxiety, depression, fear, etc., and what they will discover will be learning to "smile more frequently" (workbook, p. 284; W-pI.155.1:2). The "last step," which belongs to God whereby He reaches down and "lifts us to Himself," does not occur until we have completed all the "little steps He asks [us to] take to Him" (workbook, p. 359; W-pI.193.13:7).

In conclusion, therefore, "instant enlightenment" is not something *A Course in Miracles* teaches, just as the "holy relationship" and the "real world" are not achieved in one year. The spirituality of the Course is beyond the platitudes and postures that the ego mind conjures up. There is nothing in *A Course in Miracles* that would reinforce such misguided endeavors as instant enlightenment, achieved through being in the presence of a realized individual, instantaneous acquisitions of holy relationships, or even entering into the real world. Followers of such magical hopes will ultimately find that their efforts have come to naught, for they but reinforce more hallucinatory experiences of salvation. Indeed, it requires serious study over long years of hard work and practice to achieve the ultimate holy instant, which is the attainment of the real world.

Chapter 4

JESUS

49) Where does it say in *A Course in Miracles* that Jesus is the author, and why is there no author's name given in the book? Moreover, why are there sections on Jesus in the manual for teachers written in the third person? Is there another voice dictating here?

Almost the entire text of *A Course in Miracles* is written in the first person, where the "I" is clearly identified throughout as Jesus. Moreover, there are many places where he specifically discusses the crucifixion and resurrection. There are relatively few obvious first person references in the workbook for students and manual for teachers, but when they do occur, their impact is quite dramatic, as seen for example in workbook Lesson 70, the Introduction to the fifth review lesson, and the poem that ends the manual.

Interestingly enough, there is one section in the manual proper—"Does Jesus Have a Special Place in Healing?"—and two in the manual's appendix, the clarification of terms— "Jesus–Christ" and "The Holy Spirit"—where Jesus is spoken about in the third person. Some students have understood this shift to be a significant one that indicated that Helen was hearing another voice here. This was definitely not the case, as she was always clear that there was only one voice—Jesus—that was dictating to her. These three sections specifically deal with Jesus, and the shift in the person of the "voice" was made for stylistic purposes, *and has no other significance*. If students wish, however, they can understand these third-person sections to be the Holy Spirit speaking about Jesus.

It is in the aforementioned section in the manual for teachers where one finds this very specific statement that the source of *A Course in Miracles* is Jesus, as spoken, again if the reader wishes, by the Holy Spirit:

This course has come from him because his words have reached you in a language you can love and understand. Are other teachers possible, to lead the way to those who speak in different tongues and appeal to different symbols? Certainly there are. Would God leave anyone without a very present help in time of trouble; a savior who can symbolize Himself? Yet do we need a many-faceted curriculum, not because of content differences, but because symbols must shift and change to suit the need. *Jesus has come to answer yours.* In him you find God's Answer (manual, p. 56; M-23.7:1-7; italics ours).

The reason no author's name is given in *A Course in Miracles* is a very simple one: Jesus was quite explicit in his instructions to Helen that this be the case. Helen was also personally clear about not having her own name appear, since she was always emphatically unambiguous with people that she was not the author of the course.

50) If Jesus is the first to have accepted the Atonement for himself, as *A Course in Miracles* states, what about people like the Buddha?

This reference comes in the section in the clarification of terms called "The Holy Spirit" and states:

He [the Holy Spirit] has established Jesus as the leader in carrying out His plan [the Atonement] since *he was the first to complete his own part perfectly* (manual, p. 85; C-6.2:2; italics ours).

It would be tempting for students of *A Course in Miracles* to use this passage as a way of establishing bragging rights that "our guy" (Jesus) is better than "your guy" (Buddha, or any other enlightened teacher). But can one really believe that Jesus would indulge in such spiritual specialness? A better way to understand this passage is to recall the fact that time is not linear, and so there is nothing in *A Course in Miracles* to suggest *when* it was that Jesus accepted the Atonement for himself. And since, again, time is not linear, the whole question becomes meaningless, except for being a valuable learning opportunity in which students may release their own thoughts of specialness. It is also helpful for the student to recall that Jesus states the following, in the section in fact right before the one where the above statement appears:

> Helpers are given you in many forms, although upon the altar they are one. Beyond each one there is a Thought of God, and this will never change. But they have names which differ for a time, for time needs symbols, being itself unreal. Their names are legion, but we will not go beyond the names the course itself employs (manual, p. 83; C-5.1:3-6).

In other words, he is speaking only within a Christian framework, and so it would be inappropriate to discuss Teachers from other spiritualities, whose "names are legion."

51) If, as *A Course in Miracles* suggests, the world totally misunderstood Jesus' message two thousand years ago, why did he wait so long to correct it?

Again, this thoughtful question is based upon a linear view of time, in which two thousand years appear to be an inordinately long period of time for the error to be corrected. Clearly, the ones asking such a question are projecting onto Jesus their own impatience and, most likely, their unforgiveness of the various Christian Churches that have superimposed the ego thought system onto the ego-free teachings of the true Jesus.

A more profound way of addressing this question is to consider that being ego-free, anyone in the real world—as is Jesus —does not really choose to do anything. Having chosen the Holy Spirit once and for all, there is nothing more to choose. Therefore, there is no longer a decision maker in the mind that activates the body and interacts with the world, as is the ego's very important need. Truly advanced teachers of God— Teachers of teachers—do not *do*; they *are*. They do not plan, choose, deliberate, or behave as does a person who believes in the reality of the ego thought system. Their simple presence of love takes its shape around the needs of those who still identify with a world of form, much as water takes its shape according to the container in which it has been put, or the bed of the river shapes the flow of the water coursing through it.

In this context, therefore, we can understand that the appearance of Jesus within the world's dream two thousand years ago was the result of the Son's readiness to experience the Love of God within his dream. It is as if the mind of the Son—the only true sphere of experience there is—partially opened the door of his mind that had screened out the presence of the Holy Spirit. The mind, previously darkened by guilt, thus allowed some light in, and this light took the form of Jesus, the Son of Light, whose presence within the ego's world of darkness reminds us all that we too are children of the Light.

The fear that this light engendered—for it constitutes a grave threat to the ego's thought system of darkness—led to the Son's closing the door to protect his individual self, and this took the form of seeking to destroy Jesus and then his message, as the history of Christianity attests. This is why the gospel writers changed the entire message of Jesus and rooted it in the crucifixion, which reflected the ego's underlying plan to perpetuate its own thought system of betrayal, suffering, and death. Jesus comments on this dynamic in the Course in several places. We look at two such passages; one general to the dynamics of the Son's mind, and the other specific to Jesus himself.

> As the light comes nearer you will rush to darkness, shrinking from the truth, sometimes retreating to the lesser forms of fear, and sometimes to stark terror (text, p. 353; T-18.III.2:1).

> All who believe in separation have a basic fear of retaliation and abandonment. They believe in attack and rejection,

so that is what they perceive and teach and learn. These insane ideas are clearly the result of dissociation and projection. What you teach you are, but it is quite apparent that you can teach wrongly, and can therefore teach yourself wrong. Many thought I was attacking them, even though it was apparent I was not. An insane learner learns strange lessons. What you must recognize is that when you do not share a thought system, you are weakening it. Those who believe in it therefore perceive this as an attack on them. This is because everyone identifies himself with his thought system, and every thought system centers on what you believe you are (text, p. 98; T-6.V-B.1:1-9).

The reader should also consult "Atonement without Sacrifice" and "The Message of the Crucifixion," the opening sections of Chapters 3 and 6 in the text, for even more specific comments by Jesus about the misunderstanding of his message, and how and why it happened.

And now, two thousand years later, we see that the door to the Son's closed mind opened again to allow in the light of truth, and the result is the original message of Jesus, presented in a contemporary twentieth (soon to be twenty-first) century form. Needless to say, there have been other expressions of this light in the Christian (and non-Christian) world, but, again, we shall remain only within the context of *A Course in Miracles*.

The advantage of answering the question in this way is that one is able to avoid the anthropomorphizing of Jesus—making him think, plan, and behave the way we would—which would only once again foster the belief that we have captured him within the ego's dream, making him one of us, instead of our becoming like him. Above all, it is *always essential* to keep in mind that God has no true response to the thought of separation, even though, as we have already seen, the metaphoric language of *A Course in Miracles* often portrays it so. First and foremost, if God knew about the "tiny, mad idea," it would have had to be real. Therefore, the Holy

Spirit and Jesus—as messengers of God within the dream, and being the Voices of the plan of the Atonement which states that the dream of separation never happened—would also have to share in this non-response to error. It is Their simple light-filled presence within our minds—darkened by thoughts of sin, guilt, and fear—that help us. They *do* nothing; it is only our egos that act and react. And as long as we experience this thought of separation in the specific forms of specialness that comprise our individual lives, we must experience this Help in specific forms as well. But these forms are determined by our ego scripts, not by any specific intervention of the divine.

52) Is the Jesus of *A Course in Miracles* the same Jesus written about in the Bible, and the same person who walked the earth in Palestine two thousand years ago?

Yes, it is definitely the same Jesus who *appeared* in the world two thousand years ago, with the same message of truth —in content obviously, not form. However, it is extremely hard to believe that the Jesus of *A Course in Miracles* is the same figure written about in the Bible, just as it would be difficult to accept that the biblical Jesus resembles the truly historical one. This is not the place to delve into issues of scripture scholarship and how the gospels were written, but suffice it to state for our purposes here that the figure found in the four gospels, as well as the teachings recorded in the other books of the New Testament, are often diametrically opposed to what we find in the Course. Rather than attempt a procrustean fit of a round peg in a square hole, it seems much safer and intellectually honest for students of *A Course in Miracles* to accept that the biblical Jesus represents the collective projections of the various authors of the gospels and epistles, while the voice and person of Jesus in *A Course in Miracles* represents the ego-free being who lived and taught two thousand years ago. In conclusion, the Jesus of the Bible and the Course are mutually exclusive figures, with only the common name linking them together.

For a more thorough discussion of these differences, the reader is referred to *A COURSE IN MIRACLES and Christianity: A Dialogue.*

53) Is there a difference between Jesus and the Holy Spirit, and does it matter to whom I go for help?

The difference between Jesus and the Holy Spirit is a theological one, not a practical one. According to the Course's theory, the Holy Spirit was created by God in response to the thought of separation in His Son's mind. In reality of course, as we have mentioned several times before, such a description in *A Course in Miracles* is metaphoric, because how can God give an answer to something that never happened? At any rate, the Holy Spirit can be more properly understood as the memory of God's Love and the Son's true Identity as Christ that he carried with him into his dream. The Holy Spirit, therefore, is a *principle* or a *thought* in the Son's mind that reminds him that what he believes about himself and his Creator is false. This correction is what is known in *A Course in Miracles* as the principle of the Atonement.

Jesus, on the other hand, is a part of the Sonship, and is as tangible and specific as is the Son's belief about himself. He is the part of the Son's one mind that "remembered to laugh" at the tiny, mad idea. And therefore Jesus becomes a manifestation of the Atonement principle, or of the more abstract presence of the Holy Spirit. That is what is meant in the clarification of terms by the previously quoted statement that the Holy Spirit "established Jesus as the leader in carrying out His plan" (manual, p. 85; C-6.2:2), and by the passage in the text that is a direct reference to Jesus:

> The Atonement *principle* was in effect long before the Atonement began. The principle was love [the Holy Spirit]

and the Atonement was an *act* of love [Jesus] (text, p. 16; T-2.II.4:2-3).

On the level of practice, however, there is no difference. Both Jesus and the Holy Spirit serve as our inner Teachers, to whom we go for help in learning how to forgive. The Holy Spirit offers the student a more abstract Teacher, if Jesus is a problem; while Jesus is a more specific and personal form for the student to relate to. Either one will do, however, for Their function remains the same. Nonetheless, if Jesus is indeed a problem figure for students of his Course, then it would definitely be in keeping with the Course's very principles for such students to look at their unforgiveness of him. Thus they may explore its deeper roots so that they may be undone, just as with any unforgiveness that is present within their minds.

54) Why does Jesus repeatedly say in *A Course in Miracles* that I need to forgive him? What for?

For many students of *A Course in Miracles* this is a problematic issue. Why, they ask, do I have to forgive Jesus; I am not angry at him. I (Gloria) remember many years ago when I had my own group that met to discuss the Course. This issue was almost responsible for World War III breaking out in my dining room, where the group met every week. It was certainly not a neutral topic, and forgiving Jesus is indeed a central issue that goes to the heart of the Course's teaching about undoing the ego thought system. Let us begin our answer by looking at some representative passages from the Course where Jesus discusses this. The first two come in the section, "The Obstacles to Peace" in Chapter 19 of the text, where he states:

> I am made welcome in the state of grace, which means you have at last forgiven me. For I became the symbol of your sin, and so I had to die instead of you....
> Let me be to you the symbol of the end of guilt, and look upon your brother as you would look on me. Forgive me all

the sins you think the Son of God committed. And in the light of your forgiveness he will remember who he is, and forget what never was. I ask for your forgiveness, for if you are guilty, so must I be. But if I surmounted guilt and overcame the world, you were with me. Would you see in me the symbol of guilt or of the end of guilt, remembering that what I signify to you you see within yourself? (text, pp. 383,385; T-19.IV-A.17:1-2; T-19.IV-B.6)

And then at the beginning of the next chapter, in the section "Holy Week" which was written during the week preceding Easter, Jesus returns to this important point:

You stand beside your brother, thorns in one hand and lilies in the other [thorns and lilies are the Course's symbols, respectively, for attack and forgiveness, crucifixion and resurrection], uncertain which to give. Join now with me and throw away the thorns, offering the lilies to replace them. This Easter I would have the gift of your forgiveness offered by you to me, and returned by me to you. We cannot be united in crucifixion and in death. Nor can the resurrection be complete until your forgiveness rests on Christ, along with mine....I was a stranger and you took me in, not knowing who I was. Yet for your gift of lilies you will know. In your forgiveness of this stranger, alien to you and yet your ancient Friend, lies his release and your redemption with him (text, p. 396; T-20.I.2:6-10; 4:3-5).

Jesus has to be forgiven on two levels. The first relates to the "bitter idols" the world has made of him, which clearly reflects its projections and has nothing to do with him at all. These idols have come in both special hate and love forms, where he has either been made into a figure of judgment and punishment who demands suffering and sacrifice of his followers, or else a magical savior who, upon petition, will solve problems and reward good deeds and faithful discipleship with his love and beneficence. Once again, such images reflect the specialness needs of the image-makers, with no reference to the real Jesus at all, who clearly is beyond such ego concerns. And so it can be seen here that Jesus is to be for-given for what he has *never* done, and even more to the point, forgiven for what he has *never* been.

To the ego, Jesus is the most threatening figure imaginable, as we have already indicated in our answers to earlier questions, for if he is real, then the ego thought system cannot be. And so the part of anyone's mind that still clings to special-ness and individuality—the hallmarks of the ego thought system—would inevitably fear, and therefore attack Jesus to protect itself. This attack reflects the original ego thought that the Son of God had sinfully separated himself from the Love of God. Guilt over such attacks on Jesus—the Western world's greatest embodiment of this Love—can only lead to denial. Guilt (or self-hatred) is such an overwhelming experience that it is almost inevitably buried in our minds. This reflects the magical belief that, like the proverbial ostrich, if we do not see the problem, it is not there. This ego dynamic of avoiding the pain of our guilt culminates in projecting our belief in sin and guilt onto Jesus.

This is the meaning of the passages quoted above from the text. Rather than our accepting responsibility for our guilt—which the ego teaches us must lead to death as justified pun-ishment for our sin—we hope, once again magically, that by projecting the guilt out onto Jesus, leading to his death, we will be off the hook. For the ego would kill rather than have its existence undone. And thus two thousand years of belief in vicarious salvation, which Christian theology espouses, pro-claims that "Jesus did it for us." This insane dynamic reflects the ego's "bread-and-butter" dynamic of the guilt-attack cycle, wherein the guiltier we feel, the greater is our need to attack others in "self-defense," which in turn reinforces the guilt which always remains repressed in our minds. And then the cycle begins all over again. This is why Christians have always worshiped a slain savior, and why Catholics specifi-cally commemorate Jesus' death by reenacting it every day at Mass. Our guilt impels us continually to kill him off. And so what we forgive in Jesus is simply the projection of what remains unforgiven in ourselves.

What we find here is that this first level of forgiving Jesus for our projections onto him, is really the defense against the underlying level which reflects our real need for forgiveness: Jesus has to be forgiven for who he *truly* is. Again, if the Jesus of reality is indeed present within our minds as the perfect embodiment of God's Love—the pure expression of the Holy Spirit's Atonement principle—then our entire identity as a separated physical and psychological being is undone. It is truly *this* that we hold against Jesus. He is the living proof within the dream of our own existence, that we are wrong and he is right. He is the clear and unmistakable presence from *outside* the dream that attests to our sleeping minds that the dream itself is unreal. To accept this is to accept that we are truly not here, but dreaming a dream where we made up an individual self to replace the Self that God created. And so to preserve this made-up self, we must attack and destroy the truth. We have already examined this idea in some depth, but let us return to it once more by quoting some expressive lines from one of Helen's later poems, "Stranger on the Road," which so graphically portray this fear of confronting the truth of Jesus' existence. In effect, Jesus' presence in our minds denies the "truth" of our own thought system of fear and death, which in our strange insanity we believe is comforting to us and therefore needs to be protected from him:

> The road is long. I will not lift my eyes,
> For fear has gripped my heart, and fear I know–
> The shield that keeps me safe from rising hope;
> The friend that keeps You stranger still to me.
>
> Why should You walk with me along the road,
> An unknown whom I almost think I fear
> Because You seem like someone in a dream
> Of deathlessness, when death alone is real?

> Do not disturb me now. I am content
> With death, for grief is kinder now than hope.
> While there was hope I suffered. Now I go
> In certainty, for death has surely come.
>
> Do not disturb the ending. What is done
> Is done forever. Neither hope nor tears
> Can touch finality. Do not arouse
> The dead. Come, Stranger, let us say "Amen."
> *(The Gifts of God*, p. 103)

And so in all honesty we need to look at how we fear and hate Jesus, feelings that are almost always buried in our unconscious minds, under layers and layers of defenses. Through forgiving him for who he truly is, we learn at the same time to forgive ourselves for trying to pretend that we are *not* who we truly are, and then seeking to blame him for it. Were the presence of Jesus not so explicitly clear in *A Course in Miracles*, many students would not have the opportunity of dealing with this deeply buried layer of unforgiveness and guilt in themselves.

Chapter 5

THE CURRICULUM OF
A COURSE IN MIRACLES

55) Who gave the title *A Course in Miracles*, and why?

The title was given by Jesus. The scribing to Helen began with the words: "This is a course in miracles," and throughout the dictation this is how Jesus referred to the material. While the initial shock value of the title may attract us, and can therefore be possibly used as a justification for its use, the real reason for the title rests on the fact that the entire Course is focused on helping the student learn and understand what the miracle is, and how to apply it in one's personal life. Jesus' focus in his curriculum is on correction, specifically on how the Holy Spirit reminds us that we have a mind and that this mind is extremely powerful. It was the mind that made the problem of separation, and only it, joined with the Holy Spirit, can accept correction.

Near the beginning of the text, in fact, Jesus emphasized this point to Helen (and to all future students) in stating that the purpose of his course was to have her recognize the "power of your own thinking" (text, p. 27; T-2.VII.1:5). It is the miracle that specifically accomplishes this, by recalling to students of *A Course in Miracles* that it is their *minds* that have made up their problems (not to mention the entire physical universe), and therefore, again, it is only their minds that can change this. The miracle thus reminds us that we are the dreamers of our dreams, and that by joining with Jesus or the Holy Spirit we can accept a change from the pain that dreams have brought. As Jesus states later in the text:

> The miracle does not awaken you, but merely shows you who the dreamer is. It teaches you there is a choice of dreams while you are still asleep....

> The miracle establishes you dream a dream, and that its content is not true....
>
> The miracle returns the cause of fear to you [the mind] who made it (text, pp. 551-53; T-28.II.4:2-3; 7:1; 11:1).

56) What is the relationship of *A Course in Miracles* to other spiritual paths, and specifically to the Bible?

This is an extremely important question, because the incorrect understanding of the answer inevitably leads to serious distortion of what *A Course in Miracles* actually teaches and how it is meant to be practiced. We live in an age where many followers of spiritual paths—usually grouped together in what is termed the "new age"—emphasize unity instead of diversity. While this is an admirable spiritual goal, certainly, it does serve to deny the "fact" of our separated world; namely, that we are all different, and that different spiritual paths are thus required. Once this is accepted, then it is clear that different paths will be *different*. This is clearly obvious on one level, but is frequently obscured by the need to blur differences for the sake of a spurious unity. This does *every* spiritual path a disservice, and Jesus always made it clear to Helen personally, as well as in *A Course in Miracles* itself, how different *his* Course was from other paths. This does not necessarily mean it is better, but it does mean that it is unique.

Near the beginning of the manual for teachers, Jesus says of *A Course in Miracles*:

> This is a manual for a special curriculum, intended for teachers of a special form of the universal course. There are many thousands of other forms, all with the same outcome (manual, p. 3; M-1.4:1-2).

And we have already examined Jesus' special message to Helen—"I Need Do Nothing"—where Jesus *contrasts* his Course with other spiritualities that emphasize meditation and contemplation.

Therefore, on the one hand, the Course's relationship to other spiritual paths is that it shares the *same* goal of returning home to God. It is *different,* however, because its theology and practice are different. Jesus summarizes this relationship in his pithy comment:

A universal theology is impossible, but a universal experience is not only possible but necessary (manual, p. 73; C-in.2:5).

As we have already seen, *A Course in Miracles* is a non-dualistic spirituality, while almost all others are dualistic. Confusing the Course with other spiritual thought systems, saying "the Course is just like...(fill in your favorite spirituality)" is simply in the end a subtle ego ploy for changing *A Course in Miracles* so that its teachings will be less threatening. We, of course, have seen in our Western history a notable example of this ego device when the Christian world made Jesus and his teachings into an extension of Judaism and the Old Testament, rather than accepting him and his message as the radical gift it was, independent of all that preceded it. Students of *A Course in Miracles* should profit from this mistake of the past, and grow into the Course, rather than attempting to scale it down to their own level of understanding.

Another form of this mistake is the common practice of including *A Course in Miracles* with what Aldous Huxley termed "the perennial philosophy," a catch-all phrase used to embrace the major mystical traditions of the world. Again, this does the Course a profound disservice, because it blurs what is its distinctive contribution to the world's spiritualities: the idea that not only was the physical universe an illusion that God did not create, but that it was also "made as an attack" on Him (workbook, p. 403; W-pII.3.2:1). This profound and sophisticated psychological principle, integrated with a pure non-dualistic metaphysics is what renders *A Course in Miracles* unique among the spiritual and religious thought systems of the world.

Comparing *A Course in Miracles* specifically with the Bible, we can see four major areas of differences, making these two spiritual paths totally incompatible. We quote from the introduction to *A COURSE IN MIRACLES and Christianity: A Dialogue* by Kenneth and the Jesuit philosopher Father Norris Clarke, which explores these differences in greater depth:

> 1) *A Course in Miracles* teaches that God did not create the physical universe, which includes all matter, form, and the body; the Bible states that He did.
>
> 2) The God of *A Course in Miracles* does not even know about the sin of separation (since to know about it would make it real), let alone react to it; the God of the Bible perceives sin directly, as is portrayed in the Garden of Eden story...and His responses to it are vigorous, dramatic, and at times punitive, to say the very least.
>
> 3) *A Course in Miracles'* Jesus is equal to everyone else, a part of God's one Son or Christ; the Bible's Jesus is seen as special, apart, and therefore ontologically different from everyone else, being God's only begotten Son, the second person of the Trinity.
>
> 4) The Jesus of *A Course in Miracles* is not sent by God to suffer and die on the cross in a sacrificial act of atonement for sin, but rather teaches that there is no sin by demonstrating that nothing happened to him in reality, for sin has no effect on the Love of God; the Jesus of the Bible agonizes, suffers, and dies for the sins of the world in an act that brings vicarious salvation to humanity, thereby establishing sin and death as real, and moreover clearly reflecting that God has been affected by Adam's sin and must respond to its actual presence in the world by sacrificing His beloved Son.
>
> (pp. 2-3)

While our answer has focused on the Bible, the same basic message can be given regarding any other spiritual path. While there certainly can be nothing wrong with reading other spiritualities or being interested in learning more about them, nor in attending religious services, spiritual meetings, etc., a student of *A Course in Miracles* should at least be cautious—to make the point again—about attempting to blend together theologies or spiritual approaches that ultimately do not mix. Some spiritualities lend themselves to such "blending together"; *A Course in Miracles* does not.

57) Does the concept of the *circle of Atonement* relate to the "hundredth monkey" idea? And should "teachers of God" go out to teach *A Course in Miracles* or proselytize others?

The answer to the first question is "no"; they represent two entirely different thought systems. The "hundredth monkey" concept is based upon questionable research that concluded that there is a quantitative point that is reached in a species—like a certain weight that, once it is reached on a balancing scale, tips that portion of the scale and then that allows the remaining members of that species to acquire what the rest have already learned. *A Course in Miracles'* idea of "the circle of Atonement" is *not* a quantitative concept, and has nothing to do with accumulating numbers of students of the Course, which once this "critical mass" is reached, will save the world. We read in the manual for teachers, for example, that only *one* teacher of God is needed to save the world. This is because there *is* only one teacher—our Self. When the Atonement has been accepted by an individual, that person now remembers that there is only one Son, and therefore the dream of separation, differences, and multiplicity was simply unreal. To believe that a certain requisite number of students is needed to save the entire world clearly makes the concept of *numbers* real, not to mention establishing the reality of a species or world that has to be saved as well.

If this non-quantitative aspect of *A Course in Miracles* is not understood, then students of Jesus' Course would be tempted to believe that they must proselytize or otherwise preach the "new gospel according to the real Jesus" in order to acquire as many students of the Course as possible so that the world would be saved. As has already happened, students will band together and think of themselves as a movement, net-work, religion, church, or some such special category. They will revel in the thought that a copy of *A Course in Miracles* was sent to the Vatican, or the White House, or put in any other worldly symbol of power. They will feel drawn to criticize, judge, or attack other spiritual paths, for these must then inev-itably be seen as competitors for achieving that critical mass of people necessary to shift the balance for the salvation of the world.

All this is easily avoided by focusing *only* on what *A Course in Miracles* actually teaches, and directing one's attention *only* on one's own forgiveness lessons and the eventual acceptance of the Atonement for oneself. There *is* no one else to be "saved," and accepting this thus is our *only* responsibility.

58) Can *A Course in Miracles* be completed in one year, as the workbook seems to suggest?

This question rests on the premise that only the one-year training program of the workbook for students comprises the total mind-training (or mind-*re*training) that is the principal goal of *A Course in Miracles*. Not so. The workbook is only one aspect of a curriculum that consists of three parts: the *text*, which contains the theory and theology of the Course; the *workbook for students*, the one-year series of lessons that help the student begin the mind-training program of the Course; and the *manual for teachers,* which serves as a summary of many of the Course's teachings, as well as helping to define what Jesus means by *a teacher of God*.

Any serious student of *A Course in Miracles* recognizes that the *total* curriculum cannot in any way be completed in one year. Rather, it is a lifetime's work, and the workbook, which, again, is a specific one-year training program, is the means which would ensure that students proceed in the correct manner. Once they are in touch with their right minds and understand the process of forgiveness that the Course sets forth, students are then able to spend the rest of their lives in daily practice with Jesus or the Holy Spirit as their Teachers. As the workbook states at the end:

> This course is a beginning, not an end. Your Friend goes with you (workbook, p. 477; W-ep.1:1-2).

59) Is there a wrong or right way to practice the workbook?

There is only one rule that Jesus offers us about doing the workbook: "Do not undertake to do more than one set of exercises a day" (workbook, p. 1; W-in.2:6). Furthermore, we are urged by him to continue with our practice even if we have trouble understanding a lesson, or experience difficulty in carrying out the specific exercise because we do not believe what it says. As he comfortingly says to his students:

> Some of the ideas the workbook presents you will find hard to believe, and others may seem to be quite startling. This does not matter. You are merely asked to apply the ideas as you are directed to do. You are not asked to judge them at all. You are asked only to use them. It is their use that will give them meaning to you, and will show you that they are true.
>
> Remember only this; you need not believe the ideas, you need not accept them, and you need not even welcome them. Some of them you may actively resist. None of this will matter, or decrease their efficacy. But do not allow yourself to make exceptions in applying the ideas the workbook contains, and whatever your reactions to the ideas may be, use them. Nothing more than that is required (workbook, p. 2; W-in.8-9).

Clearly, students are encouraged in the above passage to do the workbook as Jesus gave it, one lesson at a time, in the sequence in which the lessons come. However, there is no rule against spending more than one day on a workbook lesson. Many times lessons bring up a host of related perspectives and problems in one's life, and therefore students find themselves ruminating and pondering over the personal implications of these lessons. Since the workbook is a highly personal experience for students, there cannot truly be a "right" or "wrong" way of practicing it. The correct answer, as always, is that the "right" way is practicing the workbook with the Holy Spirit; the "wrong" way is practicing with the ego. This puts the burden on the student to continue the journey with *A Course in Miracles* in as ego-free manner as possible, always maintaining a vigilance against the ego's subtle intrusions of specialness.

60) Is it necessary to do the workbook more than once?

No. The workbook for students is set up as a one-year training program, and there is no reason for a student to deviate from that. It is clear from the workbook itself, as has already been stated, that Jesus does not expect his students to complete the learning process in one year. *A Course in Miracles* is a lifetime's work, and the one-year program of the workbook— which probably should be done relatively early in a student's work with the Course, although everyone's practice with it is different—is simply to orient the student on the right path with the right teacher. Then placed in the Holy Spirit's hands, we spend the rest of our lives having Him be our Teacher of forgiveness:

> And now I place you in His [the Holy Spirit's] hands, to be His faithful follower, with Him as Guide through every difficulty and all pain that you may think is real.... Let Him prepare you further. He has earned your trust by speaking daily to you of your Father and your brother and your Self. He

will continue. Now you walk with Him, as certain as is He of where you go; as sure as He of how you should proceed; as confident as He is of the goal, and of your safe arrival in the end (workbook, p. 477; W-ep.4:1,3-6).

Very often, students' wishes to repeat the workbook (or specific lessons in an almost compulsive need to get it right) come from the desire to do it perfectly, recognizing how imperfect their willingness and practice have been. This defeats the whole purpose of the workbook, which is to train students to hear the Holy Spirit's Voice of forgiveness, instead of the ego's guilt. Indeed, one can even make the statement that the purpose of the workbook is to do it *imperfectly*, so that the mistake—labeled by the ego as a sin—of turning away from God and not placing Him first in one's life, can be forgiven and not taken seriously. Jesus' instructions to his students in Lesson 95 underscore this important goal of forgiveness. They are given in the context of students *not* doing the lessons perfectly, and choosing to forget the daily lesson in the course of the day:

Do not, however, use your lapses from this schedule as an excuse not to return to it again as soon as you can. There may well be a temptation to regard the day as lost because you have already failed to do what is required. This should, however, merely be recognized as what it is; a refusal to let your mistake be corrected, and an unwillingness to try again.

The Holy Spirit is not delayed in His teaching by your mistakes. He can be held back only by your unwillingness to let them go. Let us therefore be determined, particularly for the next week or so, to be willing *to forgive ourselves for our lapses in diligence, and our failures to follow the instructions for practicing the day's idea.* This tolerance for weakness will enable us to overlook it, rather than give it power to delay our learning. If we give it power to do this, we are regarding it as strength, and are confusing strength with weakness.

When you fail to comply with the requirements of this course, you have merely made a mistake. This calls for

117

correction, and for nothing else. To allow a mistake to continue is to make additional mistakes, based on the first and
reinforcing it. It is this process that must be laid aside, for it
is but another way in which you would defend illusions
against the truth (workbook, p. 165; W-pI.95.7:3–9:4; italics
ours).

This does not mean, certainly, that students should *not* do
the workbook a second or third time, but, as we stated in the
previous answer, they should be vigilant against their ego's
need to reinforce sin and guilt, and atone for such sin by
becoming "perfect." In other words, students should treat their
relationship with the workbook as a classroom as well; a classroom in which they bring their misperceptions to Jesus for
help and correction. In this sense, we can add a postscript to
our answer to the previous question about there being a "right
way" to do the workbook. *There is*: the "right way" is to do the
workbook the "wrong way," and then to have Jesus help you
to forgive yourself. In this way you are beginning—in the context of "forgetting" about God by "forgetting" the daily lesson
—the process of accepting forgiveness for having turned away
from God in the original instant of separation.

**61) Why do the text and workbook have different focuses,
and at times seem to be saying different things?**

Jesus refers to *A Course in Miracles* as a "multi-faceted
curriculum," and so it requires that his teaching be presented
in different forms. The text, which was dictated to Helen first,
contains the theology, metaphysical foundation, and teachings
on accepting forgiveness for our special relationships, on
which the curriculum rests. For example, only in the text—
highlighted for the most part from Chapter 15 through
Chapter 24—does one find the exposition of the teaching on
special and holy relationships. Nowhere in the workbook or
manual is this very important subject specifically discussed.
In the workbook, as Jesus explains in the introduction, the first

part (Lessons 1-220) deals "with the undoing of the way you see now," while the second part (Lessons 221-365) deals "with the acquisition of true perception" (workbook, p. 1; W-in.3:1). Nothing is mentioned about the *theory* of *A Course in Miracles*. Indeed, the specific relationship between the text and the workbook is clearly set forth in the Introduction:

> A theoretical foundation such as the text provides is necessary as a framework to make the exercises in this workbook meaningful. Yet it is doing the exercises that will make the goal of the course possible. An untrained mind can accomplish nothing. It is the purpose of this workbook to train your mind to think along the lines the text sets forth (workbook, p. 1; W-in.1).

It is *because* of these different purposes and focuses that at times the two books seem to be saying different things, and even at times seeming to contradict each other. Perhaps the best example of this interesting phenomenon relates to the role of the Holy Spirit. Many passages in the workbook urge students to ask Him for very specific help, as we can see in this example from the final lessons (361-365):

> **This holy instant would I give to You** [the Holy Spirit].
> **Be You in charge. For I would follow You,**
> **Certain that Your direction gives me peace.**

> And if I need a word to help me, He will give it to me. If I need a thought, that will He also give. And if I need but stillness and a tranquil, open mind, these are the gifts I will receive of Him. He is in charge by my request. And He will hear and answer me, because He speaks for God my Father and His holy Son (workbook, p. 476; W-p.II.361-365).

And yet we are taught in the text that it is *not* the role of the Holy Spirit to guide us in the world of *effects*—the material world of specifics—but rather to help us change our minds about the *cause* of our problems: our belief in the reality of sin and guilt. For example:

In gentle laughter does the Holy Spirit perceive the cause [the *mind's* belief in sin], and looks not to effects [the problems experienced in the physical world]. How else could He correct your error, who have overlooked the cause entirely? He bids you bring each terrible effect to Him that you may look together on its foolish cause and laugh with Him a while. *You* judge effects, but *He* has judged their cause. And by His judgment are effects removed (text, p. 545; T-27.VIII.9:1-5).

Nevertheless, if students do not understand the afore-mentioned two levels that *A Course in Miracles* is written on, and which, by the way, it never specifically identifies as such, then one is apt to conclude that these statements are contradictory. To restate these levels briefly:

Level One: the Course's metaphysical foundation, which emphasizes the difference between God and Heaven, the only reality, and the collective illusory world of the ego.

Level Two: the Course's practical level, which deals only with the illusory dream. Here, the contrast is between the wrong mind which is the ego's thought system of sin, guilt, and fear, and the Holy Spirit's correction of forgiveness within the right mind.

Regarding the subject of God, we find the same apparent contradiction. In workbook Lesson 71 we are told to ask God Himself for specific help:

> *What would You have me do?*
> *Where would You have me go?*
> *What would You have me say, and to whom?*
> (workbook, p. 121; W-pI.71.9:3-5)

Moreover, all of Part II of the workbook consists of prayers from the student *to* God the Father. This is so, despite the following very clear statement—interestingly enough, also from the workbook—that God does not hear our prayers:

> Think not He hears the little prayers of those who call on Him
> with names of idols cherished by the world. They cannot
> reach Him thus (workbook, p. 335; W-pI.183.7:3-4).

And in the manual for teachers we read these lines about the
true nature of our words:

> God does not understand words, for they were made by sepa-
> rated minds to keep them in the illusion of separation. Words
> can be helpful, particularly for the beginner, in helping con-
> centration and facilitating the exclusion, or at least the con-
> trol, of extraneous thoughts. Let us not forget, however, that
> words are but symbols of symbols. They are thus twice
> removed from reality (manual, p. 51; M-21.1:7-10).

Clearly, the first passage has us asking God the Father a
series of specific questions to which we would fully expect to
receive answers. Part of the reason it is framed this way is that
inherent within the separation thought is the statement that I
am self-created, and therefore am my own source. So by asking God for help at what we have referred to as Level Two, the
level of the illusory dream, I am acknowledging that I am not
an autonomous self-created being, but rather someone who
needs help in undoing this false self that I made up. It is in this
way that the thought that I am on my own has been undone,
and I realize that the answers to all my questions have already
been given, and that they are one. As *A Course in Miracles*
emphasizes, the Holy Spirit's correction to my ego's dream of
separation has already occurred, because time is already over,
as we have noted in a previous chapter (question 16 on
page 25). But since I walk around believing and experiencing
otherwise, the correction will reach me in a form to which I
can relate.

In conclusion, from these two examples alone it should be
clear that Jesus indeed knew what he was doing when he dictated these three books of *A Course in Miracles*, and it is we
who lack the understanding of how he integrates his curriculum and accomplishes the goal of changing our thought
system.

62) Does *A Course in Miracles* have to be studied, or is it enough just to do the workbook and read the text randomly, in whatever way I feel guided to do?

Again, there is no right or wrong in pursuing *A Course in Miracles* as a spiritual path. However, there are certain guidelines we can present that can help ensure that one's work with the Course is *not* being guided by the ego. One such guideline is always to return to Jesus' own instructions for his curriculum. The three books are set up as a college course, in which, to summarize this again, there is the basic *textbook*, which contains the theoretical material that the instructor (here of course it is Jesus) wishes the class to study, learn, and understand; the *workbook*, which as in a laboratory course for example, is the practical application of what is learned in the text; and the *manual*, which offers guidelines for all pupils, who in this curriculum are also teachers.

What does this mean for Course students? Simply, that they are asked by Jesus to *study, learn, and understand* his teaching material, as well as to *practice* the Course's principles of forgiveness. That is why, for example, he does not require that students *understand* what is said in the workbook, as we have already seen in the quotation cited above (page 115). But he does not let his students off that hook when it comes to the text. Near the end of Chapter 1, he states very clearly:

> This is a course in mind training. All learning involves *attention and study* at some level. Some of the later parts of the course rest too heavily on these earlier sections not to *require their careful study.* You will also need them for preparation. Without this, you may become much too fearful of what is to come to make constructive use of it. However, *as you study these earlier sections,* you will begin to see some of the implications that will be amplified later on (text, p. 13; T-1.VII.4; italics ours).

In fact, during the Course's dictation, Jesus was quite insistent to Helen and Bill that they *study these notes*, as he referred to the material. He was speaking in the manner of a college professor insisting that his students pay careful attention to what was being taught, *and to study the lecture notes he was giving*. It would be in direct contradiction to the wishes of Jesus *not* to study the text, as he specifically asks. To ignore these very *specific* instructions at the end of Chapter 1 provides still another example of students' authority problems, wherein they believe that they know better than Jesus what is in their own best interests, not to mention how they should proceed with *his* Course.

Regarding the workbook, since it is not meant to be the *teaching* aspect of the curriculum, it need not be read nor studied in the manner that the text should be. Certainly, however, it needs to be practiced as the instructions indicate. This being said, we nonetheless believe that students would do well in their work with *A Course in Miracles*—to enhance their understanding of it—to read carefully through the workbook itself at some point after they have gone through the lessons, as they would do with the text. Many would be astounded at what they would find there: a depth of teaching that can easily be overlooked as one does the lessons in the one-year training program.

63) Should children be taught *A Course in Miracles*?

Helen herself was fond of saying about *A Course in Miracles*: "Finally, there is a spiritual system for the intellectual." It would seem to us that the only way children could be taught the Course is by their parents, teachers, etc., living it. As we know, children have the burden on their young shoulders of learning a vast amount of information related to coping with physical, psychological, and social demands within a world of multiplicity. To try to teach them that this is a world of illusions and dreams—all made as an attack on God—is to not only confound this learning, but to confuse them about how to relate to this world. Therefore, the wish to have a children's version of the Course misses the whole point of the Course. What makes *A Course in Miracles* what it is, is the integration of its teachings on forgiveness with its non-dualistic metaphysics. Without that foundation you no longer have *A Course in Miracles.*

To be sure, it is always helpful to teach children in words and deed that God is a loving Creator Who does not punish His children. And there are many spiritualities that teach this which are perfectly adaptable for children. *A Course in Miracles* on the other hand, cannot be so adapted without losing its essence. However, those adult figures who relate to children and are students of the Course can help them undo the ego thought system that concludes with the premise that God will punish them because of their sins. Since parents and other authorities are the inevitable dream figures symbolizing God, they have the capacity to reinforce either the ego's thought system of guilt and punishment, or the Holy Spirit's thought system which corrects mistakes through forgiveness.

64) According to *A Course in Miracles*, how should children be reared?

As the Course states: "The curriculum is highly individualized, and all aspects are under the Holy Spirit's particular care and guidance" (manual, p. 67; M-29.2:6). Therefore, *A Course in Miracles* does not teach any specific behavior at all, including how to rear children. But what the Course does teach is that if you are a parent, or someone who works with children, it is incumbent on you to ask continuously for the help of the Holy Spirit. In that way, everything you think and do and say will be coming from your right mind, and not your ego.

Many students of *A Course in Miracles* have related to us that once they started studying the Course, they were reluctant to make judgments about their children's behavior, or even to discipline them out of fear of making judgments about them and telling them they were wrong. This is a distortion of what Jesus is teaching. Primarily, one can understand that being a parent or working closely with children is a very intense classroom that we have chosen, precisely because of the constant judgments that need be made about what is in the child's best interest—decisions a child is not capable of knowing—when the child will clearly choose something that will be hurtful to it. As Jesus states in the text:

> Babies scream in rage if you take away a knife or scissors, although they may well harm themselves if you do not (text, p. 52; T-4.II.5:2).

Secondly, learning how to get oneself out of the way in order to access the right mind, and perhaps disciplining a child by saying—*without guilt or anger*—"No, this behavior will not be tolerated," can be very important landmarks in the process of one's own growth.

Therefore, as with anything else, there is no right or wrong way of rearing children, no specific way according to *A Course in Miracles*. There is only the individual's way of asking the Holy Spirit's help in practicing forgiveness. His Love is always the same, and finds its particular expression through each particular individual in each particular circumstance. Our responsibility is to remove, with His help, our ego's interferences so that we may be more directly guided by this Love—in *all* relationships, with children or adults.

65) What about groups that meet on *A Course in Miracles*?

Let us begin with the statement that there is absolutely nothing in *A Course in Miracles* about groups, meeting with other people, or joining together on the level of form, etc. The significance of this is that it illustrates how the process of studying the Course occurs on the level of the mind, and is in truth a self-study course. Its emphasis is always on joining with Jesus or the Holy Spirit, *in the mind*, and asking Their help to perceive differently a seemingly external relationship, or any situation for that matter. This is the meaning of forgiveness. Our *experience* of being in a body, interacting with other bodies, becomes the classroom in which we ask our Teacher to help us change our *minds*. The only joining then that is truly meaningful is with Jesus or the Holy Spirit, and that should *always and only be* the Course student's focus, what in the text is referred to as "The Greater Joining" (text, pp. 555-57; T-28.IV). Since, as is stated in the section with that title, the Holy Spirit is in all the minds of the separated Sons, by joining with Him—which, again, is the true meaning of forgiveness—one has *already* joined with everyone. The actual words from the text are:

> The Holy Spirit is in both your minds [you and your brother], and He is One because there is no gap that separates His Oneness from Itself. The gap between your bodies matters not, for what is joined in Him is always one (text, pp. 556-57; T-28.IV.7:1-2).

Thus it is irrelevant for the purposes of forgiveness that there be or not be a "gap between bodies." We are already joined. Forgiveness undoes the *seeming* gap that exists between our minds, and returns to our awareness the fact of our oneness with each other and with our Source.

All too often students of *A Course in Miracles* forget this greater joining, and because of the good feeling that so often comes from externally being with others, they feel that *this* is what Jesus is talking about when he discusses joining. In truth, however, his focus is always on the *removal* of the barriers of specialness that we have placed between ourselves and others. And these barriers are always thoughts within our wrong minds, as the Holy Spirit is a Thought within our right minds. And so our attention should always be placed on bringing the ego's thoughts of specialness to the Holy Spirit's thoughts of forgiveness—once again, within the mind. Only then can we be sure that our external joining with others is truly of Him and not the ego.

Certainly, there can be nothing wrong with any student of *A Course in Miracles* joining externally with other students. However, the focus of Course students cannot be behavior, but always the inner teacher whom we choose to guide our behavior. Therefore, the bottom line is to try as best as possible to have our actions—whether they involve studying the Course, or anything else—originate in the sincere attempt to bring our ego involvement to Jesus *before* engaging in the activity.

If students feel led to be a part of some sort of Course group or organization, they should always be vigilant that such involvement does not become a substitute for their own individual work—study and practice—with the material itself. Otherwise, they will easily fall into the lap of specialness, which can be defined, as we saw earlier, as using anything as a substitute for the Love of God. To make our opening point again, there is a reason for Jesus saying nothing at all in the Course about joining together in groups. And students should always be mindful of his sole emphasis in *A Course in Miracles*, which is on the individual student's relationship with the Holy Spirit, based upon the willingness to practice forgiveness.

66) I have need for a psychotherapist, but I only want a therapist who is a student of *A Course in Miracles*, or at least is familiar with it and sympathetic to its teachings. What should I do?

As a therapist, I (Kenneth) am frequently asked by Course students around the country to recommend a therapist who is a student of *A Course in Miracles*. My response is usually something to the effect of: "If you require surgery, would you want someone who is a Course surgeon, or someone who is a fine surgeon?" Similarly, what *any* person wants who requires therapy is someone who is well trained and supervised, and is a person that can be related to and trusted. There are relatively few students of *A Course in Miracles* who meet these qualifications of a psychotherapist, when compared to the majority of professional therapists that are available. Simply being a student of the Course and "asking" the Holy Spirit for guidance to help others is hardly sufficient, especially given the amount of specialness that is usually present in such "therapists," a situation we have commented on before.

Therefore, if a student of the Course finds a professional therapist who is also a student of *A Course in Miracles*, all well and good. But if that student truly needs a sensitive and competent psychotherapist, a therapist's lack of background in the Course should hardly be a consideration against choosing such a therapist for oneself. Students seeking therapy should be wary of "training programs" in psychotherapy that are run by non-professional Course students, who then recommend these "trainees" to others; or those who have referral lists of "Course therapists." Once again, you do not want a person to cut open your stomach who has been trained by other students of the Course, but rather a trained and competent surgeon who has been trained by other trained and competent physicians. It should not be any different in choosing a therapist to help with a personal problem. Legitimate training programs in psychotherapy may not be free from the ego's thought system, as Jesus points out in the pamphlet "Psychotherapy: Purpose, Process and Practice" (p. 18; P-3.II.2:2-4), but they at least guarantee a certain amount of training and supervised experience that form a solid foundation of expertise that ensures that the patient is in competent professional hands. One can be very effectively helped to overcome ego blocks by a therapist who is not a student of *A Course in Miracles*, or of any other spiritual path for that matter.

67) If *A Course in Miracles* **is a universal teaching, why did it come in such sectarian (i.e., Christian) terms? Doesn't that limit its worldwide applicability?**

While the basic message of *A Course in Miracles* is universal—"God's Son is guiltless, and in his innocence is his salvation" (manual, p. 3; M-1.3:5)—its form certainly is not, nor is it meant to be. We have already quoted Jesus' words to the effect that this is a "special curriculum," which clearly reflects that it has a special audience: the Western world that has grown up under the strong influence of Christianity and 20th-century psychology, an influence that has not been very Christian nor spiritual. This is why the Course's language is so Western, and, more specifically, Christian and psychodynamic in statement. As the specific spiritual path we call *A Course in Miracles*, the Course is simply not meant to have worldwide applicability. Other cultures and religious traditions have, and will continue to have their own spiritual paths, just as we in the Western world now have the Course, among many others. As we have repeatedly pointed out in this book, the universal joining with all people is the *content* of the universal course, but the specific ways in which people learn this lesson constitutes the *forms* of the "special curriculum," of which *A Course in Miracles* is simply one example. Forms, almost by definition, are not the same and cannot blend together. Therefore they *cannot* be universal, or for all people. This is why Jesus teaches in the introduction to the clarification of terms, to repeat and extend this important statement:

A universal theology is impossible, but a universal experience is not only possible but necessary. It is this experience toward which the course is directed (manual, p. 73; C-in.2:5-6).

This "universal experience," it goes without saying, is love, and *A Course in Miracles* is but one form of regaining it.

68) Why is the language of *A Course in Miracles* so difficult to read and understand? Why couldn't Jesus have written it more simply?

It is always a temptation for followers of spiritual paths to change the original inspiration and make it what *they* think it should be, rather than the way it was given. And the same phenomenon occurs with *A Course in Miracles* as well. Rather than adopting an attitude of acceptance of what is, and then adapting to *it*, students are tempted to make the *Course* adapt to them. This is the case with the style of writing one finds in *A Course in Miracles*, which at times seems to many students to be dense, elliptical, obscure, and simply too difficult to understand.

However, there is a reason for the Course's style, and it would be doing Jesus' pedagogy a great disservice to want to change it. *A Course in Miracles* is written in such a way that it demands that its students pay very careful attention to what is written. This is not a book—and we are speaking primarily here about the text—that can be speed-read. Almost all students have experienced the necessity to read the same sentence several times before beginning to understand it; or have agonized over the proper subjects of the pronouns. But what they usually find, if they are faithful to Jesus' purpose, is that through the very *process* of figuring out the meaning of a sentence or passage, they have uncovered a level of meaning they would otherwise not have received. The "careful study" that Jesus urges for his students, discussed above, is meant very literally. And the writing style ensures that serious students will give Jesus the attention and dedication he is asking for. Once students of the Course understand its teachings, they will be astounded as to how "simple, clear, and direct"— words Jesus himself uses to describe his Course—*A Course in Miracles* truly is.

69) Can *A Course in Miracles* be done by myself, or do I need to have a partner?

As we have already mentioned, *A Course in Miracles* is inherently a self-study curriculum. One's life—past, present, and anticipated future—is the classroom. All one's relationships—whether falling into any of the three categories given in the manual ranging from superficial through a circumscribed intense relationship, to a lifetime one (manual, pp. 6-7; M-3)—provide the "partners" needed for the practice of forgiveness. One does not need a partner "designated" for such practice, nor does the partner have to be a student of the Course, as we discussed briefly in question 31. Anyone and everyone will do. To insist that one's partner be spiritually like-minded, and even more specifically, a student of *A Course in Miracles*, is to confuse form with content, and to fall into the trap of specialness that is the very thing the Course aims at undoing. As we discussed previously, the Course's definition of *joining* has nothing to do with bodies or externals of any kind—"Minds are joined; bodies are not" (text, p. 359; T-18.VI.3:1). *Joining*, rather, has to do with joining with Jesus or the Holy Spirit, in Whom are all members of the Sonship found as one, regardless of their spiritual path, or absence of it.

Therefore, it does not really matter with whom one practices the lessons of forgiveness. Projection of guilt remains what it is, *regardless* of the form of the relationship or the nature of the person or situation on whom it is projected. Everyone and everything in the dream we call our lives offers the opportunities for recognizing that what we have perceived and made real outside our minds, has existence only *within* our minds. Therefore, nothing else is required for one's work with *A Course in Miracles* except one's life as the classroom, and the willingness to have Jesus teach us how to perceive it differently.

70) Is *A Course in Miracles* best practiced in seclusion, without worldly distractions?

Upon serious consideration of this question, one would recognize that it makes no sense. Within our individual dreams we are always alone, because there is no world outside our minds. To attempt to separate ourselves from the world, to move apart from it, is simply to fall into the ego's trap of "making the error real" that we have already discussed. We would have again seen the problem as being outside the mind —in this case the busy and distracting world of separation and multiplicity—and would have therefore made it real, ensuring that it will never be undone. In truth, however, the problem is the busy and distracting *thoughts* of separation and multiplicity that are in our minds. By changing the outer world to solve the problem of our inner world is a good working definition of what the Course means by *magic*. And so, by students believing that they can only study and learn *A Course in Miracles* by leaving the classroom of their lives, they are almost certainly following the guidance of their egos which would see to it that they would never learn their lessons of forgiveness; they had unknowingly separated themselves from them.

While there are always exceptions, we think it is a fair statement to make that almost all students of *A Course in Miracles* should practice its principles right where they are. That is why Jesus included the following question in the manual for teachers: "Are Changes Required in the Life Situation of God's Teachers?" His answer explains that for the majority of students, "it is most unlikely that changes in attitudes would not be the first step in the newly made teacher of God's training" (manual, p. 25; M-9.1:4). And those who are guided to change their situations "almost immediately," are "generally special cases" (manual, p. 25; M-9.1:6). Naturally, many students of *A Course in Miracles* think they fall into that *special* category. Most people's lives are painful ones, filled with circumstances, relationships, and bodily conditions that are quite traumatic. It is difficult therefore for them to avoid the temptation to reinterpret the Course, or to "hear" the Holy Spirit "tell" them to leave their jobs and/or families, and simply be with Him to learn and teach the Course to others. It is always helpful to remember that there can be no "worldly distractions" unless you first wanted to be distracted, and therefore had a need that this be so. As Jesus states in the text in the context of evil:

> Forget not that the witness to the world of evil cannot speak except for what has seen a need for evil in the world (text, p. 540; T-27.VII.6:2).

The world, like the body, in and of itself is neutral. It simply does for us what we ask it to do for us.

We frequently like to remind students about the origins of *A Course in Miracles*. It did not begin in a desert, or a holy mountaintop, nor was Helen a cloistered nun, "buried alive for God." Jesus dictated his Course to Helen in the midst of a very stormy professional relationship with Bill, where both of them were quite busy in their hectic jobs at one of the world's largest, most prestigious, and most ego-based medical centers, in the heart of what is among the world's most important and busiest cities. One's "training is always highly individualized" (manual, p. 25; M-9.1:5), yet we believe that *A Course in Miracles'* very history provides a solid witness and example for how its students should apply their little willingness to learn it in the midst of their normal, everyday lives.

71) Have there been people who have successfully completed *A Course in Miracles* (and are in the real world), and who are they?

When this is asked during workshops, we sometimes tell people (with a straight face) that there is a list, but we keep it locked in a safe in the office. In truth, however, this is a question no one could truly answer, for how would one know? To begin with, the chances are that someone who is truly in the real world would not go around broadcasting the fact. Second, people usually think of "success" in the Course in terms of certain external criteria that can be seen, and these criteria would clearly not be shared by everyone. One of our favorite stories to illustrate this last point is the earnest young man who came up to Kenneth after a week-end workshop in a midwestern city saying: "I know you must be a very advanced person, because you don't smoke cigarettes, don't drink coffee, and don't keep running to the bathroom." Other criteria of "spirituality" include not locking one's car door or house because one "trust[s] my brothers, who are one with me" (workbook, pp. 329-30; W-pI.181), or giving up insurance policies because one "place[s] the future in the Hands of God" (workbook, pp. 360-61; W-pI.194). The point naturally is that such judgments about spiritual advancement are always based on externals, without the one who judges knowing what the content is behind the form, regardless of the form's "spiritual" appearance.

Moreover, implicit in questions like this is a latent fear of being unable to achieve the Course's goal. Hearing about others who have often can provide the external witness, when Jesus' expressed confidence in his students is not enough.

The bottom line, whenever one is tempted to indulge in such thoughts of spiritual specialness, is always to focus on one's own Atonement lessons, thereby avoiding the distraction of thinking of others who have or have not "made it." As peace returns to the student's mind, the question will already have departed from it.

72) What should one say to a stranger, family member, or friend who asks what *A Course in Miracles* is?

Basically, there is no wrong or right way to answer this question, whether it be a stranger, family member, or friend that is asking about the Course. Ultimately, everyone must go within and try to get the ego self out of the way, and then ask for help in how to respond. Specifically, one should pay careful attention to any of the various forms of ego specialness that would interfere in speaking to others about *A Course in Miracles*. These include: 1) feeling oneself to be important because one is associated with such a spiritually advanced teaching that comes from Jesus himself, and therefore one wants the listeners to be impressed, if not depressed because they are not Course students; 2) discomfort related to the figure of Jesus, both as the author of *A Course in Miracles* as well as its central figure; and 3) discomfort related to the Course itself—its religious and distinctively Christian and patriarchal language, not to mention its radical teachings which include the key metaphysical principle that God did not create the physical or material universe.

Therefore, while there are no correct or incorrect words to use in talking about *A Course in Miracles*, there *is* a correct way to proceed. And this entails asking Jesus or the Holy Spirit for help in getting one's ego out of the way so that the most loving words will flow through us. In truly letting Them be the Guides for speaking, one can be sure that the Course's integrity will be maintained, and at the same time one is free to be sensitive to the needs and level of understanding of the person being spoken to. Here, as elsewhere, we can see that the process is always the same, regardless of the specific situation. That is why Jesus repeatedly speaks of his Course as being simple.

Index to *A Course in Miracles* References

INDEX

INDEX

Foundation for *A Course in Miracles*®
Teaching Organization of the Foundation for Inner Peace

Academy ✦ Retreat Center

Kenneth Wapnick received his Ph.D. in Clinical Psychology in 1968 from Adelphi University. He was a close friend and associate of Helen Schucman and William Thetford, the two people whose joining together was the immediate stimulus for the scribing of A COURSE IN MIRACLES. Kenneth has been involved with the Course since 1973, writing, teaching, and integrating its principles with his practice of psychotherapy. He is on the Executive Board of the Foundation for Inner Peace, publishers of A COURSE IN MIRACLES.

Gloria Wapnick has a Masters degree in History from Hunter College (1970), and taught social studies in a New York City high school, where she was also Dean of Students. Gloria has been working with A Course in Miracles since 1977, and conducted her own group for several years.

In 1983, Kenneth and Gloria began the Foundation for A COURSE IN MIRACLES, and in 1984 this evolved into a Teaching and Healing Center in Crompond, New York, which was quickly out-grown. In 1988 they opened the Academy and Retreat Center in upstate New York. In 1995, they began the Institute for Teaching Inner Peace through A COURSE IN MIRACLES, an educational corpo-ration chartered by the New York State Board of Regents. The Insti-tute is under the aegis of the Foundation, administering workshops and Academy courses. The Foundation also publishes a quarterly newsletter, "The Lighthouse," free of charge. The following is Kenneth and Gloria's vision of the Foundation and description of the Center.

In our early years of studying *A Course in Miracles,* as well as teaching and applying its principles in our respective professions of psychotherapy, and teaching and school admin-istration, it seemed evident that this was not the simplest of thought systems to understand. This was so not only in the intellectual grasp of its teachings, but perhaps more impor-tantly in the application of these teachings to our personal lives. Thus, it appeared to us from the beginning that the Course lent itself to teaching, parallel to the ongoing teachings of the Holy Spirit in the daily opportunities within our relationships which are discussed in the early pages of the manual for teachers.

One day several years ago while Helen Schucman and I (Kenneth) were discussing these ideas, she shared a vision that she had had of a teaching center as a white temple with a gold cross atop it. Although it was clear that this image was symbolic, we understood it to be representative of what the teaching center was to be: a place where the person of Jesus and his message in *A Course in Miracles* would be manifest. We have sometimes seen an image of a lighthouse shining its light into the sea, calling to it those passers-by who sought it. For us, this light is the Course's teaching of forgiveness, which we would hope to share with those who are drawn to the Foundation's form of teaching and its vision of the Course.

This vision entails the belief that Jesus gave *A Course in Miracles* at this particular time in this particular form for several reasons. These include:

1) the necessity of healing the mind of its belief that attack is salvation; this is accomplished through forgiveness, the undoing of our belief in the reality of separation and guilt.

2) emphasizing the importance of Jesus and/or the Holy Spirit as our loving and gentle Teacher, and developing a personal relationship with this Teacher.

3) correcting the errors of Christianity, particularly where it has emphasized suffering, sacrifice, separation, and sacrament as being inherent in God's plan for salvation.

Our thinking has always been inspired by Plato (and his mentor Socrates), both the man and his teachings. Plato's Academy was a place where serious and thoughtful people came to study his philosophy in an atmosphere conducive to their learning, and then returned to their professions to implement what they were taught by the great philosopher. Thus, by integrating abstract philosophical ideals with experience, Plato's school seemed to be the perfect model for our teaching center.

We therefore see the Foundation's principal purpose as being to help students of *A Course in Miracles* deepen their understanding of its thought system, conceptually and experientially, so that they may be more effective instruments of Jesus' teaching in their own particular lives. Since teaching forgiveness without experiencing it is empty, one of the Foundation's specific goals is to help facilitate the process whereby people may be better able to know that their own sins are forgiven and that they are truly loved by God. Thus is the Holy Spirit able to extend His Love through them to others.

A teacher is defined in the Course as anyone who chooses to be one, and so we welcome to our Foundation all those who wish to come. We offer lectures and workshops for large groups as well as courses for smaller groups that would facilitate more intensive study and growth.

The Foundation, about 120 miles from New York City, is situated on ninety-five acres surrounding beautiful Tennanah Lake in the Catskill Mountains. Its country location and comfortable accommodations provide a peaceful and meditative setting in which students may carry out their plans for prayer, study, and reflection.

RELATED MATERIAL ON *A COURSE IN MIRACLES*

By Kenneth Wapnick, Ph.D.

Books and Pamphlets

CHRISTIAN PSYCHOLOGY IN *A COURSE IN MIRACLES*. Second edition, enlarged. Discussion of the basic principles of the Course in the context of some of the traditional teachings of Christianity. Includes a new Preface and an Afterword.
ISBN 0-933291-14-0 • #B-1• Paperback • 90 pages $4.
Audio tape of the first edition of the book, read by Kenneth Wapnick
#B-2 $5.

PSICOLOGÍA CRISTIANA EN *UN CURSO DE MILAGROS*. Spanish translation of CHRISTIAN PSYCHOLOGY IN *A COURSE IN MIRACLES*. Includes a glossary of some of the more important terms used in the Course.
ISBN 0-933291-17-5 • #B-1s • Paperback • 114 pages $5.

A TALK GIVEN ON *A COURSE IN MIRACLES*: An Introduction. Fifth edition. Edited transcript of a workshop summarizing the principles of the Course; includes the story of how the Course was written.
ISBN 0-933291-16-7 • #B-3 • Paperback • 160 pages $4.

UNA INTRODUCCIÓN BASICA A *UN CURSO EN MILAGROS*. Spanish translation of A TALK GIVEN ON *A COURSE IN MIRACLES*: An Introduction. Includes a glossary of some of the more important terms used in the Course.
ISBN 0-933291-10-8 • #B-3S • Paperback • 152 pages $4.

BETRACHTUNGEN ÜBER *EIN KURS IN WUNDERN*. German translation of A TALK GIVEN ON *A COURSE IN MIRACLES*: An Introduction. Order from: Greuthof Verlag und Vertrieb GmbH • Herrenweg 2 • D79261 Gutach i. Br. • Germany • Tel. 07681-6025 • FAX 07681-6027.
ISBN 0-933291-12-4

GLOSSARY-INDEX FOR *A COURSE IN MIRACLES*. Fourth edition, revised and enlarged. A study guide: summary of the Course's theory with a listing of all major terms; glossary of 139 terms and index of most important references; index of more than 800

scriptural references as found in *A Course in Miracles*, cross-referenced to the Bible. The book is keyed to both the first and second editions of the Course.
ISBN 0-933291-03-5 • #B-4 • Hardcover • 734 pages $20.

FORGIVENESS AND JESUS: The Meeting Place of *A Course in Miracles* and Christianity. Fourth edition. Discussion of the teachings of Christianity in the light of the principles of the Course, highlighting the similarities and differences; the application of these principles to issues such as injustice, anger, sickness, sexuality, and money.
ISBN 0-933291-13-2 • #B-5 • Paperback • 355 pages $16.

THE FIFTY MIRACLE PRINCIPLES OF *A COURSE IN MIRACLES*. Third edition. Combined and edited transcript of two workshops; line-by-line analysis of the fifty miracle principles, with additional material.
ISBN 0-933291-15-9 • #B-6 • Paperback • 115 pages $8.

LOS CINCUENTA PRINCIPIOS DEL MILAGRO DE *UN CURSO EN MILAGROS*. Spanish translation of THE FIFTY MIRACLE PRINCIPLES OF *A COURSE IN MIRACLES*.
ISBN 0-933291-19-1 • #B-6s • Paperback • 139 pages $8.

AWAKEN FROM THE DREAM. Gloria and Kenneth Wapnick. Presentation of the Course's major principles from a new perspective. Includes background material on how the Course was written.
ISBN 0-933291-04-3 • #B-7 • Paperback • 133 pages $10.

THE OBSTACLES TO PEACE. Edited transcript of tape album; line-by-line analysis of "The Obstacles to Peace"—sections central to the Course's theory—and related passages.
ISBN 0-933291-05-1 • #B-8 • Paperback • 295 pages $12.

LOVE DOES NOT CONDEMN: The World, the Flesh, and the Devil According to Platonism, Christianity, Gnosticism, and *A Course in Miracles*. An in-depth exploration of the non-dualistic metaphysics of *A Course in Miracles*, and its integration with living in this illusory world.
ISBN 0-933291-07-8 • #B-9 • Hardcover • 614 pages $25.

A VAST ILLUSION: Time According to *A Course in Miracles*. Second edition. A weaving together of various passages from the Course to present a coherent statement of time, including its metaphysical nature, the role of the miracle and forgiveness in collapsing time, and finally the end of time. (Edited and expanded transcription of the tape album "Time According to *A Course in Miracles*.")
ISBN 0-933291-09-4 • #B-10 • Paperback • 343 pages $12.

ABSENCE FROM FELICITY: The Story of Helen Schucman and Her Scribing of *A Course in Miracles*. Discussion of Helen's lifetime conflict between her spiritual nature and her ego; includes some of her recollections, dreams, letters, and personal messages from Jesus—all never before in print; an account of her own experiences of Jesus, her relationship with William Thetford, and the scribing of the Course.
ISBN 0-933291-08-6 • #B-11 • Paperback • 521 pages $16.

OVEREATING: A Dialogue. An Application of the Principles of *A Course in Miracles*. Pamphlet presenting the Course's approach to issues such as food addiction and preoccupation with weight. (Edited and slightly expanded version of the tape "Overeating.")
ISBN 0-933291-11-6 • #B-12 • Paperback • 35 pages $3.

A COURSE IN MIRACLES AND CHRISTIANITY: A DIALOGUE. Kenneth Wapnick and W. Norris Clarke, S.J. Discussion identifying the radical differences as well as the similarities between the thought systems of the Course and biblical Christianity. Topics discussed include: The Origin of the World; Jesus: Nature and Role, The Meaning of the Crucifixion and the Resurrection; The Eucharist; and Living in the World.
ISBN 0-933291-18-3 • #B-13 • Paperback • 113 pages $5.

Video Tape Albums

SEEK NOT TO CHANGE THE COURSE. Reflections on *A Course in Miracles*. Talk given by Gloria and Kenneth Wapnick, including questions and answers, on some of the more common misunderstandings about the Course.
#V-1 135 mins. VHS $30 PAL (non-US) $40
Audio tape version $15.

FOUNDATION FOR *A COURSE IN MIRACLES* Conference and Retreat Center. Gloria and Kenneth Wapnick speak about the Course's beginnings, the origin and purpose of the Foundation, and their vision of its development in the future. A visual and verbal portrait of the Center.
#V-2 24 mins. VHS $10 PAL (non-US) $20.

THE REAL WORLD (Three-hour unedited workshop). Gloria and Kenneth Wapnick. Explanation of the process of attaining the real world beginning with the metaphysics of *A Course in Miracles* and the undoing of the ego by the Holy Spirit. The culmination of this process is the real world—the state of mind in which both the problem and the answer disappear, leaving only the memory of God's Love, exemplified in our world by Jesus.
ISBN 0-933291-99-X #V-3 3 hrs. VHS US $30 PAL (non-US) $40.

THE REAL WORLD (Two-hour edited workshop). Gloria and Kenneth Wapnick. Edited version of the video listed above. Interspersed throughout the workshop are excerpts of an interview with Gloria and Kenneth. Audience questions have not been included in this version.
ISBN 0-933291-98-1 #V-4 VHS US $20 PAL (non-US) $30.

AN INTERVIEW WITH KENNETH AND GLORIA WAPNICK. A one-hour interview conducted by Corinne Edwards at the Miracle Network in Chicago in December 1995. Topics discussed include: Helen Schucman and her experience of writing down *A Course in Miracles* as dictated by Jesus; Kenneth's experience with the Course and his relationship with Helen Schucman and William Thetford; the nature of the Course, its core teachings and their contrast with Christianity; the application of the principles to specific life situations; common misunderstandings of the principles and mistakes made in applying them.
#V-5 • 1 hr. • VHS (US) $15.

Audio Tape Albums
Classes and Workshops

CHRISTIAN PSYCHOLOGY IN *A COURSE IN MIRACLES*. Audio tape of first edition of book of the same title, read by Kenneth Wapnick.
ISBN 0-933291-50-7 • #B-2 • 1 tape $5.

THE SIMPLICITY OF SALVATION. Intensive overview of the Course. The two levels of discourse in the Course; in-depth summary of the major principles; comparison of the Course and Christianity; the story of how the Course was written.
ISBN 0-933291-51-5 • #T-1 • 8 tapes $48.

HOLY IS HEALING. Psychotherapeutic applications of the Course. Workshop weaving together the theory of *A Course in Miracles* with psychotherapeutic and personal examples offered by participants.
ISBN 0-933291-52-3 • #T-2 • 8 tapes $48.

ATONEMENT WITHOUT SACRIFICE: Christianity, the Bible, and the Course. Workshop exploring the relationship between *A Course in Miracles* and the Judaeo-Christian tradition, with special emphasis placed on the role of sacrifice and suffering.
ISBN 0-933291-53-1 • #T-3 • 2 tapes $10.

THE END OF INJUSTICE. Overview of the Course. The thought systems of the ego and the Holy Spirit; application of principles to problems involving sex, money, injustice, and sickness.
ISBN 0-933291-54-X • #T-4 • 6 tapes $36.

THE EGO AND FORGIVENESS. Introductory overview of the Course. The ego's thought system of sin, guilt, fear, and special relationships, and its undoing through the Holy Spirit's thought system that includes forgiveness and holy relationships. (Album consists of first two tapes of "The End of Injustice.")
ISBN 0-933291-55-8 • #T-5 • 2 tapes $10.

THE FIFTY MIRACLE PRINCIPLES OF *A COURSE IN MIRACLES*. Line-by-line commentary on the fifty miracle principles which begin the text; introduces students to the central concepts of the Course: Atonement, miracles, healing, time, forgiveness, the Holy Spirit.
ISBN 0-933291-56-6 • #T-6 • 3 tapes $18.

THE WORLD ACCORDING TO *A COURSE IN MIRACLES*. The Course's theory of the world and its role in the ego's plan to usurp God's function and substitute a world of its own for the creation of God.
ISBN 0-933291-57-4 • #T-7 • 3 tapes $18.

THE OBSTACLES TO PEACE. Line-by-line commentary on the "Obstacles to Peace" sections of the text, focusing on the ego's attraction to guilt, pain, and death, and the fear of God's Love, and the undoing of these obstacles through forgiveness.
ISBN 0-933291-58-2 • #T-8 • 6 tapes $36.

SPECIAL RELATIONSHIPS—PART 1. Line-by-line commentary on sections discussing specialness; explains the unloving nature of most relationships, and how to transform them.
ISBN 0-933291-59-0 • #T-9 • 8 tapes $48.

SPECIAL RELATIONSHIPS—PART 2. Continuation of Part 1, developed through commentary on later chapters in the text including "The Healed Relationship," "The Treachery of Specialness," "The Forgiveness of Specialness."
ISBN 0-933291-60-4 • #T-10 • 6 tapes $36.

TIME ACCORDING TO *A COURSE IN MIRACLES*. The metaphysics of time—its holographic though illusory nature; the relation of time to the role of the miracle in the plan of the Atonement; the end of time.
ISBN 0-933291-61-2 • #T-11 • 6 tapes $36.

JESUS AND *A COURSE IN MIRACLES*. Discussion of passages in the Course in which Jesus refers to himself: as the source of the Course; his historical teaching example as the manifestation of the Holy Spirit, and perfect model of forgiveness; and his role as our teacher, without whom the undoing of the ego's thought system would be impossible.
ISBN 0-933291-62-0 • #T-12 • 5 tapes $30.

CAUSE AND EFFECT. The importance of this principle in understanding how forgiveness undoes the ego's thought system of guilt and punishment; line-by-line analysis of text sections on our dreams of suffering and victimhood.
ISBN 0-933291-63-9 • #T-13 • 8 tapes $48.

PSYCHOTHERAPY: PURPOSE, PROCESS AND PRACTICE. Line-by-line commentary on the companion pamphlet to the Course, scribed by Helen Schucman from Jesus.
ISBN 0-933291-64-7 • #T-14 • 7 tapes $42.

THE GIFTS OF GOD. A discussion of the inspired poetry of Helen Schucman, scribe of the Course; includes personal reminiscences about Helen.
ISBN 0-933291-65-5 • #T-15 • 3 tapes $18.

SEEK NOT TO CHANGE THE COURSE: Reflections on *A Course in Miracles*. Gloria and Kenneth Wapnick. Audio version of video tape of the same name.
ISBN 0-933291-66-3 • #T-16 • 2 tapes $10.

LOVE DOES NOT OPPOSE. Gloria and Kenneth Wapnick. The importance of non-opposition as the basis of forgiveness in special relationships.
ISBN 0-933291-67-1 • #T-17 • 8 tapes $48.

THE SONG OF PRAYER. Line-by-line commentary on the companion pamphlet to the Course, scribed by Helen Schucman from Jesus; the role of prayer as a reflection of the process of our acceptance of the true meaning of Jesus' presence in our lives; Jesus' relationship with Helen as the model for understanding the nature of prayer.
ISBN 0-933291-68-X • #T-18 • 10 tapes $60.

THE ORIGIN OF *A COURSE IN MIRACLES*. The story of the scribing of *A Course in Miracles*; reflections on Helen Schucman and William Thetford.
ISBN 0-933291-69-8 • #T-19 • 1 tape $6.

I WILL BE STILL AN INSTANT AND GO HOME. A collection of two talks and a meditation by Kenneth Wapnick, and one talk by Gloria Wapnick and Kenneth—given at various Sunday services.
ISBN 0-933291-70-1 • #T-20 • 1 tape $6.

JESUS AND THE MESSAGE OF EASTER. The Course's view of Jesus, and the meaning of his crucifixion and resurrection.
ISBN 0-933291-71-X • #T-21 • 8 tapes $48.

THE AUTHORITY PROBLEM. The authority problem with God and its reflection in our everyday life.
ISBN 0-933291-72-8 • #T-22 • 5 tapes $30.

OUR GRATITUDE TO GOD. Our gratitude to God, Jesus, and to each other; the obstacles and resistances to this gratitude.
ISBN 0-933291-73-6 • #T-23 • 5 tapes $30.

SICKNESS AND HEALING. Discussion of the cause and purpose of sickness in the ego thought system; analysis of healing as occurring in the mind—the healing of the belief in guilt, by turning to the Holy Spirit and forgiving.
ISBN 0-933291-74-4 • #T-24 • 8 tapes $48.

WHAT IT MEANS TO BE A TEACHER OF GOD. Discussion of the ten characteristics of a teacher of God; also includes discussion of magic and healing.
ISBN 0-933291-75-2 • #T-25 • 6 tapes $36.

OVEREATING: A DIALOGUE BASED UPON *A COURSE IN MIRACLES*. The ego dynamics involved in food addictions and weight problems; forgiveness through the Holy Spirit as the solution.
ISBN 0-933291-76-0 • #T-26 • 1 tape $6.

TO JUDGE OR NOT TO JUDGE. The Course's teachings on judgment; the process of recognizing our need to judge, and letting Jesus or the Holy Spirit judge for us.
ISBN 0-933291-77-9 • #T-27 • 4 tapes $24.

HEALING THE UNHEALED HEALER. The characteristics of the unhealed healer; healing through joining with Jesus in understanding all forms of sickness and problems as calls for love.
ISBN 0-933291-78-7 • #T-28 • 8 tapes $48.

THE REAL WORLD: OUR HOME AWAY FROM HOME. A discussion of our true home in Heaven, the ego's home in the world, and the Holy Spirit's correction of the ego's world: the real world.
ISBN 0-933291-79-5 • #T-29 • 8 tapes $48.

TRUE EMPATHY: THE GREATER JOINING. The world's version of empathy contrasted with the Holy Spirit's true empathy.
ISBN 0-933291-80-9 • #T-30 • 8 tapes $48.

JESUS: THE MANIFESTATION OF THE HOLY SPIRIT. A discussion of Jesus and the Holy Spirit in the context of the difference between appearance and reality, and the importance of Jesus as our guide in leading us out of the dream; includes a discussion of the relationship of Jesus to Helen Schucman and to *A Course in Miracles*.
ISBN 0-933291-81-7 • #T-31 • 5 tapes $30.

THE LAWS OF CHAOS: OUR WAR WITH GOD. An in-depth exploration and discussion of the five laws of chaos that form the foundation of the ego's thought system, and powerfully express the ego's defenses against the Love of God.
ISBN 0-933291-82-5 • #T-32 • 12 tapes $72.

"THERE MUST BE ANOTHER WAY." The words that led to the birth of *A Course in Miracles* provide the theme of this workshop which discusses forgiveness as the "other way"—rather than specialness—of relating to ourselves, each other, and to God.
ISBN 0-933291-83-3 • #T-33 • 1 tape $6.

THE METAPHYSICS OF SEPARATION AND FORGIVENESS. Summary of the teachings of *A Course in Miracles*, specifically showing how the principle that the thought of separation and the physical world are illusions becomes the foundation for the understanding and practice of forgiveness in our daily lives.
ISBN 0-933291-84-1 • #T-34 • 1 tape $6.

THE WORKBOOK OF *A COURSE IN MIRACLES*: ITS PLACE IN THE CURRICULUM—THEORY AND PRACTICE. Discussion of the metaphysical principles underlying the lessons, the mind-training aspects of the workbook, Jesus' gentle teaching method, and students' common misuses of the workbook. Two charts and an annotated outline of the workbook included.
ISBN 0-933291-85-X • #T-35 • 8 tapes $48.

MAKING THE HOLY SPIRIT SPECIAL: THE ARROGANCE OF THE EGO. Presentation of the major Course teachings on the role of the Holy Spirit—and Jesus as His manifestation—and the importance of Their Presence in our lives. Discussion of the contrasting attitudes of arrogance and humility in asking help of the Holy Spirit, as well as what it means to hear His Voice. The idea that the Holy Spirit acts in the world is shown to rest on misunderstandings of the principles and language of the Course, as well as on our unconscious desire for specialness.
ISBN 0-933291-86-8 • #T-36 • 7 tapes $42.

THE MEANING OF JUDGMENT. Discussion based on "The Forgiving Dream" from the text, centering on four forms of judgment: 1) the dream of judgment against ourselves; 2) looking with Jesus at this ongoing judgment of guilt without further judgment; 3) judging all things in accord with the Holy Spirit's judgment; 4) joining with Jesus in the judgment of God's Love that is the only reality.
ISBN 0-933291-87-6 • #T-37 • 1 tape $6.

THE WEB OF SPECIALNESS. The metaphysical basis of specialness as an attack on God and as a defense against our true Identity as His Son, followed by a detailed explanation of the intricacies and subtleties of specialness in the context of a commentary on sections from Chapter 24 in the text. A discussion of the process of identifying the pervasive and insidious patterns of specialness in all areas of daily life, the fear, resistance, and deception encountered in this process, and the process of forgiving our specialness through the willingness to join with Jesus in looking at it honestly and without judgment.
ISBN 0-933291-88-4 • #T-38 • 12 tapes $72.

DUALITY AS METAPHOR IN *A COURSE IN MIRACLES*. A comprehensive study of what is to be taken literally and what is to be taken metaphorically in *A Course in Miracles*, and the distortions that result from not recognizing this difference between symbol and fact—explained in the context of the metaphysics of duality and separation, and what Jesus teaches about the world, joining, forgiving, prayer, the Holy Spirit, himself, and the only reality: the non-dualistic oneness of God and Christ.
ISBN 0-933291-89-2 • #T-39 • 8 tapes $48.

RULES FOR DECISION. A line-by-line analysis of the seven rules for decision from the section "Rules for Decision" in Chapter 30 of the text. A comprehensive study of the Course's concept of decision making, and discussion of what it means to choose Jesus, rather than the ego, as our teacher.
ISBN 0-933291-90-6 • #T-40 • 8 tapes $48.

I WANT THE PEACE OF GOD. A commentary on passages from Lesson 185, "I Want the Peace of God," and from "What Is the Peace of God?" in the manual for teachers. The commentary focuses on the idea that to say and mean the words "I want the peace of God"

reflects the willingness to look openly with Jesus at our secret wish *not* to be peaceful. Only by choosing against our desire to attack can our decision to be peaceful have meaning, allowing the peace of God to be our only reality.
ISBN 0-933291-91-4 • #T-41 • one tape $6.

FORGIVING JESUS: "Stranger on the Road." Discussion of our need to forgive Jesus because he is right and we are wrong about ourselves. The context is Helen Schucman's poem "Stranger on the Road," which expresses her experiences of the crucifixion and the resurrection, and reflects her conflicts—shared by practically all students of the Course—in developing a relationship with Jesus.
ISBN 0-933291-92-2 • #T-42 • 2 tapes $10.

THE BIBLE FROM THE PERSPECTIVE OF *A COURSE IN MIRACLES*. Kenneth and Gloria Wapnick. A presentation of the Bible and the Course as mutually exclusive spiritual paths, demonstrating that attempts to graft the Bible on to the Course result in the distortion and corrution of the meaning of both systems. The Course, with its non-dualistic God, and Jesus who teaches Atonement without sacrifice, is presented as the correction of the biblical thought system.
ISBN 0-933291-93-0 • #T-43 • 6 tapes $36.

THE THEOLOGY OF *A COURSE IN MIRACLES*. Kenneth and Gloria Wapnick. A presentation of the unique non-dualistic theology of *A Course in Miracles* contrasted with the dualistic theology of Judaism and traditional Christianity. The workshop focuses on the Course's radically different teachings on God, Jesus, sin, salvation, and Atonement, and the importance of these for the practice of forgiveness.
ISBN 0-933291-94-9 • #T-44 • 2 tapes $10.

THE INHERITANCE OF GOD'S SON. Kenneth and Gloria Wapnick. A line-by-line commentary on this important section from the text of *A Course in Miracles*. Discussion of the ways in which, through guilt and blame, we obscure our inheritance as God's perfect sinless creation, and the undoing of these defenses by joining with Jesus through forgiveness of ourselves and others.
ISBN 0-933291-95-7 • #T-45 • 2 tapes $10.

THE SIGN OF CHRISTMAS IS A STAR. Kenneth and Gloria Wapnick. The theology of Christmas discussed in the context of two radically different views of Jesus: traditional Christianity which portrays him as the only Son of God, special and different from everyone else, sent by God to atone for the sins of humanity; *A Course in Miracles*, in which Jesus presents himself as the reflection in our minds of the light of Heaven, reminding us of our true reality as the sinless children of God, the Identity of Christ we all share as one.

ISBN 0-933291-96-5 • #T-46 • 2 tapes $10.

THE HOLY CHRIST IS BORN IN ME TODAY. Kenneth and Gloria Wapnick. The world's veneration of Jesus' birth explained as the reinforcement of the ego's specialness, which always seeks to substitute idols for the true God. This approach is contrasted with that of *A Course in Miracles*, in which Jesus teaches that the acceptance of his presence is but the rebirth in awareness of our oneness as Christ, the true meaning of Christmas.

ISBN 0-933291-97-3 • #T-47 • 2 tapes $10

FROM TIME TO TIMELESSNESS. Originally a lecture given as an introductory overview to an Academy course held at the Center in October 1995. It summarizes the role that time plays in the ego's strategy of protecting its individuality through its thought system of sin, guilt, and fear, which translates in the world of form as past, present, and future. The role of Jesus in undoing our belief in time, retracing our steps up the ego's ladder and returning us to our true home in eternity, is also discussed.

ISBN 0-933291-49-3 • #T-48 • 2 tape $6

See next page for ordering information

Ordering Information

For orders *in the U.S. only*, please add $3.00 for the first item, and $1.50 for each additional item. Most orders are shipped UPS. However, orders to *P.O. Boxes, Alaska, Hawaii*, and *Puerto Rico* are shipped Fourth Class Parcel Post (add an additional $1.00 per item for First Class Mail).

New York State residents please add local sales tax. (New York law requires sales tax on shipping and handling charges.)

For *international orders*, please send in order and VISA or MasterCard number, and postage will be added to the charge for the order. We can ship ground or air. Please specify!

VISA and MasterCard accepted.

Order from:

Foundation for *A Course in Miracles*®
1275 Tennanah Lake Road • Roscoe, NY 12776-5905
(607) 498-4116 • FAX (607) 498-5325

* * * * *

A COURSE IN MIRACLES and other scribed material
may be ordered from:

Foundation for Inner Peace
P.O. Box 598 • Mill Valley, CA 94942
(415) 388-2060

A COURSE IN MIRACLES, Second edition:

Three volumes: Hardcover $40

One volume (complete): Hardcover: $30

One volume (complete): Softcover: $25

*PSYCHOTHERAPY: PURPOSE, PROCESS AND PRACTICE: $3.00

*THE SONG OF PRAYER: PRAYER, FORGIVENESS, HEALING: $3.00

THE GIFTS OF GOD: $21.00

*These two pamphlets are also available combined in one softcover volume entitled *Supplements to A COURSE IN MIRACLES. Order from:*
Viking/Penguin: 1-800-526-0275 • FAX 1-800-227-9604
Penguin USA: 120 Woodbine Street • Bergenfield, NJ 07621

Additional copies of this book may be ordered from:

Foundation for *A Course in Miracles*®
1275 Tennanah Lake Road
Roscoe, NY 12776-5905

Send a check or money order (in US funds only) for $8.00 plus
shipping: please see preceding page for shipping charges.

I am interested in receiving a newsletter ☐

I am interested in receiving a catalog of books and tapes ☐

I am interested in receiving a schedule of workshops and classes ☐

Place me on your mailing list to receive your annual catalog and quarterly newsletter ☐

PLEASE PRINT NEATLY

Name _____

Address _____

_____

City, State, Zip _____

Foundation for *A Course in Miracles*
1275 Tennanah Lake Road
Roscoe, NY 12776-5905

Place
postage
here